Dear Self

Ryan Weems

Contents

Introduction..4

Chapter I
Who are you? Finding yourself....................7-14

Chapter II
Root problems...15-21

Chapter III
Insecurities & Pain....................................22-32

Chapter IV
Where does understanding dwell..............33-40

Chapter V
Your foundation (Relationships)................41-47

Chapter VI
Purpose Filled...48-56

Chapter VII
Pain in your purpose (The Valley).............57-66

Chapter VIII
Sacrifice a Little for a Lot..........................67-70

Chapter IX
Cup of Focus & Pinch of Faith...................71-77

Chapter X
Accountability...78-87

Chapter XI
The Value of Appreciation........................88-91

Chapter XII
Releasing Your Emotions..92-96
Chapter XIII
Limitless Boundaries..97-102
Note From The Author..103

Introduction

If you are reading this now I would like to welcome you to a book of positivity and love. That means you are here because you want to improve your life, impact the world in a positive way, or find your purpose. In today's society it can be very difficult to stay positive with so much negativity going around. Sometimes it seems no matter what we do the world continues to get worse. Where does the real change begin? If you want me to be honest, the real change starts with us. Every single day we wake up, we should look ourselves in the mirror and ask ourselves, "How can I be better today?" "How can I make the world a better place starting with me?" "How can I make a positive impact in society?" I believe we go through similar problems that we all can relate too regardless of race, religion, ethnicity, influence, & upbringing. I'd like to welcome you to the mind of a young man stepping into his late 20's that will give you a different perspective of life. Not only to share my own personal story, but to also use my story & perspective as a tool to help make a positive impact on the world. Before you continue to read, I warn you that this book may take you on an emotional rollercoaster where it will force you to re-live painful moments in your life but it will also take you on an energetic journey of love and positivity. There is this saying I hear at least once a year where an adult would give me some amazing advice and they follow that statement up with "I wish someone gave me this information I'm sharing with you, my life would be a lot easier". Well this book is advice, gems, lessons, information, perspective, perception, and many more all in one. Have an open mind, sit back, and enjoy this beautiful journey you are about to embark because once you start this is no turning back. All love and positivity.

DEAR SELF

(Ryan Weems)

PUBLISHED BY: (Ryan Weems)
Copyright © 2018 All rights reserved.

No part of this publication may be copied, reproduced in any format, by any means, electronic or otherwise, without prior consent from the copyright owner and publisher of this book.

I
Who are you? (Finding Yourself)

If you haven't asked yourself this question, now would be an excellent time to ask. Who am I? Yes, my name is Ryan Weems. Yes, I am 26 years old. Yes, I love many things - but who am I really? When I first asked myself this question, I had no real answer, but I knew who I wanted to be. I wanted to be whoever my peers were going to accept me as but still within my moral code. Being accepted is something we all want growing up right? The need to feel wanted and accepted by our peers could become so great that we are willing to make decisions beyond our moral compass, just so we won't feel out of place. I've seen women bully their own friends just to be accepted by new friends. I've seen guys play women just to get a high five from the guys but deep down I knew they didn't want to do it. The need to feel wanted and accepted overpowered what they truly wanted to do.

Is that who we really are, though? Would we fake who we truly are just to live a life that isn't true to ourselves? Well, I can tell you from not only observation but personal experience that I have faked who I truly was to fit in.

DEAR SELF

Growing up without my father present in the household or any male role models around at a very young age, I didn't know who to emulate. "Who am I supposed to be like? If I can't be like my dad, I'll turn to my next best thing which is NBA players." Basketball was #1 in my life at the time. I watched nothing but basketball and cartoons growing up so who was my role model at the time? Allen Iverson. He was everything I wanted to be as a kid, from the baggy clothes, to the fancy crossovers, to the "do it my way" attitude and even putting cornrows in my head. That's who I chose to act like during my younger stage in life. As I got older and went into middle school, I was still on my search to find out who I was, so I started listening to more rap music and my favorite rapper at the time was T.I. So guess who I tried to emulate at this point? I'm sure you guessed right. This was around the time I lived in Miami with a Southern accent, so I began to talk like T.I., dress like T.I., put my hat to the side of my head like him and even put on the tough guy front.

Now, I'm not saying it's something wrong with those guys but that just wasn't who I was. I was lost because I didn't know who I was growing up as a young kid. Although I emulated them, I didn't feel like the genuine me. If you ever have to force yourself to act like someone else, that alone is a sign that it's not the real you. The real you should feel natural and comfortable. I didn't feel comfortable with myself which is why I took on so many other people's personalities. At the time, I was unaware of who I was, so I acted out my role models personalities. Not just the rappers and NBA players but even my cool friends, as well. I would take pieces of their personality that I thought were cool and tried to mix them with mine. Deep down, I was battling an identity crisis of who I truly was and who I wanted to be for acceptance and just comfort within myself. I was already at a disadvantage with my height because I was a "late bloomer" and I was always shorter than the average person in my younger stages. I felt as though I needed to make up for my physical appearance by adding other qualities to my personality such as being intelligent or funny.

The only thing that never changed about me is my sense of humor and I'd like to think that's a gift. As I got older and went to college, I was still lost about who I wanted to be. Many of my teammates on the basketball team were from New York so I picked up a lot of their lingo, saying words like "Yo B" and "son". Pretty funny now that I think about it, but I even began to dress like them with the skinny jeans, fitted hats, and book bags loose on my back. These were the "cool kids" in my eyes and I still was on a mission to find out who I truly was. Not having my father around, I chose to act like my peers in the hopes of finding myself. I'll never know if having my father in the house would have solved all of my identity questions/wonderings, but what I do know is that I was missing my father and I was missing that male guidance. In trying to create my identity, I even tried to emulate both of my uncles. Out of all the males in the world, those were the two I wanted to be like the most. Those were the cool males that I started to look up to as role models when I hit my late teenager stages. To this day my uncles are still my role models but I am my own person, so I continue to search for who I am.

Fast forward to my early twenties where I began to find bits and pieces of myself. I started to get more comfortable with who I was and I started to care less about what people thought about me. I will say, that was a huge step for me because me not caring about others opinions allowed me to start being more comfortable with the pieces of myself that I was afraid to share with the world. I stopped caring about being the cool guy and cared more about being comfortable with myself. Now, was I 100% comfortable? Not at all, but not caring about people's opinions was at least the first step for me in finding myself. I began to listen to videos on manhood and one person that helped me with learning a lot about myself was Steve Harvey. I would listen to his morning show every day on the way to work and although it was very entertaining, he also gave great advice from the perspective of a man and that's what I was searching for. His words were valuable to me because not only did a lot of what he said make sense to me, but it aligned with a lot of my values. I was so interested in his morning show that I would sneak and listen to it while at work with one headphone in my ear, ducking and dodging my boss. Once I began to develop my own ideas and make my own decisions, I began to realize little by little who I was. See, not caring about what people thought about me allowed me to dress how I wanted to and not try to fit in. It allowed me to listen to the music I liked around whoever I was around. I made up my mind that either you will accept me for who I am or I'm fine with not being your friend. Becoming myself or Finding my own identity allowed me to be around like-minded people who had the same intentions and goals that I had.

Fast forward to 2015 which was a rough year for me. I lost one of my best friends, my grandmother to cancer. She was someone who accepted me and loved me with all of her heart and was the person who introduced God into my life. She planted that seed of God early on in my life to the point where no matter what I did or how far I got off my path with my spirituality, I never forgot God. She laid the foundation early in my life to where I knew if things got traumatic in my life, I knew exactly who to run to. When I lost my grandmother that was the first death in my family so not only did I experience losing a loved one for the first time, but I lost someone who meant everything to me. I got to a point where I felt so low and so lost that all of those people I practiced being over the years could do nothing to change or fix how I felt. Losing a loved one is painful, whether you know yourself or not but losing my grandmother combined with the pain of me not knowing who I was, I felt even more lost. Life didn't make sense to me anymore nor did the world I lived in. With my cloudy mental state, I hit rock bottom.

All this time, over 25 years, and I still didn't know who I was in my entirety. I became so lost. I had no choice and used what my grandmother taught me. I turned to God in my darkest hour and prayed until I got answers. That's when I truly began the journey of me finding my true self as a man. As months would go by, God revealed many things about myself that were old and new, showing me my true self. I was loving every bit of it. The journey was extremely difficult, but I appreciated it because I was so focused on become my true self, I didn't worry about the bumps in the road to get there. When I started analyzing people and realized how lost the majority of us are due to not knowing who we truly are, I realized we live lives of confusion, clutter, and we travel down a dark road that leads to many dead ends. Men were in the streets because of no father figure, bad influence, or poor choices. Women were finding love from the wrong men, acting out like people from reality shows, or emulating their lost parents. I realized that what both males and females had in common was an identity crisis.

In order for you to find your true self, you must seek God wholeheartedly. All of these years, I never bothered to ask God who I was but when I took that step, my life changed in a major way. He began to show me who I was, not only through my unique personality, but he revealed to me new gifts about myself that I never realized and combined what he showed me with his word. To this day, I feel the potential of who I am supposed to be. All of the dots start to connect and life began to make sense once you start the process of finding yourself. You begin to fall in love with the person you truly are. Once you begin the process of loving yourself, your perception of everything becomes different. The little things that used to matter that you would lose sleep over won't matter anymore. You will start to develop different ideas, new interests, the way you value yourself will change, and the world becomes much clearer. You begin to have more compassion for others, you attract more positive people. I can go on and on about the process but trust me, it is a beautiful journey. A journey that I am currently still on.

Am I where I need to be? Absolutely not. But the journey that I am on is amazing and what God has shown me about myself so far is so genuine and so comfortable, that I feel at home within myself. My name is Ryan Weems and I love basketball, but I discovered I love writing more. I enjoy helping others, and although I love God with all my heart, I am not perfect but I am maximizing my effort to be better every day. I love kids, I enjoy learning, I have a soft spot for people who are considered the underdogs in life, and I am still insecure about certain things. I enjoy intelligent conversations and I am a huge fan of love. I am family oriented, I love animals, I enjoy giving surprises, I am funny, and I am a father. I slip up from time to time and sin, but I will not let that stop my mission to find myself and get closer to God. In that list, I not only wanted to share the good things about myself but the bad as well because we are human and have flaws. It is about the commitment and effort we put into what is important in our lives that matters and what's important to me is my purpose, finding my true self, self-love, and getting close to God.

If I could offer advice that helped me continue on this journey it is that you MUST have patience because God takes his time to fix you. It won't take a few months, it won't take a year, it will take a very long time so you need to have patience with God and yourself. The second piece of advice is you must stay committed to what you set out to do. You will be tempted to go back to old friends and your old lifestyle out of habit, but you have to stay committed and focused on the long term goal. Patience and Commitment are the two main things that kept me on the straight path. As I mentioned, I've slipped up a few times, but I never got discouraged because I knew I had to be patient with myself and stop at no cost to reach my goal to become better. This is just the beginning of my search of finding my true self and for those who want to find themselves, seek God wholeheartedly and he will order your footsteps. I will say this journey is probably the most difficult challenge I have ever faced in my life. There will be many tears, many lonely days ahead of you, many heartaches, doubts and fears. You will lose friends, loved ones, and be very lonely because you cannot take everyone on the journey to where you are going. You may not get answers to your questions immediately as to why you are going through such a rough time, but you will get answers at some point and I promise it will all be worth it when you get to the finish line. Think about it like a race - give every ounce of energy and commitment to your running and don't worry about how tired you are. Yes, you might be tired at the finish line but once you catch your breath the reward will all be worth it. All you have to do is be willing and 100% committed to the journey and watch what God does for your life.

"Sometimes you can't find your purpose until you find yourself" – Ryan W.

II
Root problems

This is one of the most important subjects for EVERYONE to understand, because this is an issue we all have in life. As you know, experiences and certain events throughout life shapes and molds us into who we are. There are reasons as to why we act the way that we do. For example, when you encounter a person who lashes out at other people for no reason it is probably because they are hurt about a past experience that they never healed from. Sometimes, these experiences affect us deeply and we do not know how to release or handle it. I have heard of women who are sleeping around with many men throughout their lifetime because they are looking for the love that they never received from their father. Now I am not saying that this is always the case, but it has been known to be a contributing factor as to why they chose to make that decision. I have also witnessed women lashing out at men because they were molested or raped when they were younger. Therefore, their perception of men is already tainted from that traumatic experience. The same concept applies to men. I know men who are always accusing women of cheating because they were cheated on in a prior relationship. I have also seen men become arrogant and conceited because they were bullied or called ugly their entire lives. What they have managed to do is mask their pain and insecurity with designer clothes, shoes, or expensive cars.

Well, that is what I refer to as your root problem. We all have situations where we have had or currently have root problems. Have you ever stopped to ask yourself what is your root problem? What is the foundation of all your problems? Where did it start? Believe it or not, your root problem has some type of connection to all of your problems and can start at any moment in your life and at any age. The thing with root problems is sometimes we allow it to live within us for so long that later in life we do not realize that it affects our core being. It can literally dictate our personality, character, behavior and decision making process. For example, if you have an issue with your behavior in certain situations you may realize that you need to change. In order for you to change your behavior, you have to go to the foundation of all of your problems.

There are several reasons why some people never fix their root problem. One obvious reason is that they are unaware that they have a problem in the first place. Lack of self-awareness gives that person the illusion that nothing is wrong with them in the first place. Lack of self- awareness is also very dangerous because you will never accept responsibility for yourself. You will always blame other people for your decisions, and continue along the path of hurting others and yourself. Another reason that people do not want to fix their root problem is because it is too painful to relive the memory that caused the trauma in the first place. Although I do understand that it causes a tremendous amount of pain that is the only way for you to resolve the issues associated with your root problem.

To give you a visual, imagine you have a giant tree growing in your front yard. The entire yard represents your life and the giant tree represents your problems. Let's say for example you were molested as a child. The root of the tree would be the sexual assault. As the tree grows it develops a trunk which is fear. Then the tree sprouts a variety of branches such as distrust, bitterness and hatred. Let me share my own story to provide a better explanation. My relationship with my father was my root problem. Our relationship was inconsistent due to the fact that he was in and out of my life. Therefore, my father not being there was the root problem to my tree. The tree grew a tree trunk that I label distrust. The reason why I had such distrust because I felt that if I cannot trust my father to be there, then who could I really trust? If a parent could do this to their own child, then others are capable of doing anything to you. I began to have a natural distrust for people which grew into many other problems such as jealousy, bitterness, anger, unforgiving, being distant, and confusion. I call these my branches because they all stemmed from the trunk of my tree, which was distrust.

Let's take a closer look at some of those branches: I would be envious of other kids who had fathers in their life. If I saw a kid playing catch with his dad, I would become jealous because I did not have moments like those with my father. I then became unforgiving. I felt as though my father had no excuse for not being around, therefore I did not want to forgive him at any cost. I was also confused because I just could not understand why my father did not want to be around me every day or not make an effort to do all of the things that he needed to do. Those branches turned into twigs which represents how I extended my problems onto other people. Because I was jealous, bitter, angry hurt and confused, I took it out on other people.

The final parts of the tree are the leaves. The leaves represent the consequences of how the health of my tree affected myself and others. See, what many do not realize is when you are hurting other people, you are really hurting yourself. You may not even be aware that you are doing so. You do so by pushing away people who love you, you ruin relationships, and you are adding water to a tree that already has unhealthy roots. In order for us to fix our other problems you must attack the root problem head on. You have to face your fears and relive that pain. Whether it is through a conversation, therapy, or releasing it to God and letting him order your foot steps to fix your root problems. When you come to the realization of your root problem, I challenge you to grab a piece of paper and draw a tree. At the root of the tree I want you to write your root problem. At the trunk of tree, I want you to label the biggest affect that came from your root problem. For your branches (you can make as many as you need), I want you to label the problems that stem from your trunk. For your twigs, I want you to label how it has affected other people. For the leaves, label how you felt once you realized the effects it had on others.

After you have drawn your tree, find a place to put it up such as a wall or you can hide it if you do not want anyone to see it yet. Every day, take a look at the paper and visualize you chopping that tree down from the bottom. It is a process chopping down your tree, so be patient and consistent. Once you have chopped the tree down, pat yourself on the back because you have tackled the hardest part. Although the root is still in the ground it is okay because the tree is no longer growing. Also remember that the yard is labeled as your life so you still have the tree (your problems) in your yard to clean up. Now that you got the hard part out the way you can start cutting away at the trunk, then to the branches, twigs, and finally the leaves. Once you have finished clearing up the debris, your life will start to improve. Remember that this can be a long process, especially if you have had years of pain. Ten or twenty years of problems will not be fixed in a few months or even a year. Be patient with yourself, endure that pain caused it will be very difficult and stay consistent. I promise it is worth it once your tree is cut and your yard is clean.

Another very important step that is very necessary in your process of clearing the debris is that you have to be willing to approach it with an open heart. You have to be willing to not only listen and accept it but it is necessary for you to be forgiving. I know forgiving people is not easy to do but sometimes forgiving is not for the other person but for yourself. As I stated on my tree, I was unforgiving at a point in time and the unforgiveness adding more problems to my life. Sometimes people have this big misconception of "forgiving" because people think saying I forgive you is actually forgiving someone. Sorry to inform you, but that is only partially true. Reason being is that I'm sorry is just the word and first step to an apology. That is the point where you are acknowledging and taking responsibility that you have made a mistake. The best apology is changed behavior. Saying I'm sorry or I forgive you can only be validated if it is followed by an action. For example, if your partner has cheated on you and apologized but continue to cheat then they are not truly sorry. When people apologize and continuously do the same thing, all that means is that they acknowledge the action but does not care to fix it.

When expecting change, there must be some consideration given according to the problem. For example, if you have a partner that has had issues with their attitude for 30 years you cannot expect immediate change. It is a long process, so the important thing to look at is their action, effort, and improvement. It is possible that they will probably explode or slip back into old behavior patterns. During those times it is important to focus on the important things. The same concept applies for forgiveness. When you are in search of forgiving whoever hurt you with your root problem, you must also follow that forgiveness with action. If you say that you forgive the person who hurt you, but continue to talk about past transgressions every time that you get into an argument, then you did not forgive them. No one is asking you to forget what they did to hurt you. It is natural to remember what happened, but throwing it in their face or always bringing it up is not forgiving the person wholeheartedly. You are deluding yourself and the person who you claim that you forgive. Always remember that forgiveness is an act of self-healing. As I stated before my father was the root to my problems but because I faced my problem head on and addressed everything our relationship is a million times better now and that was what I was aiming to accomplish. Not only did our relationship get fixed but I learned more about my father and what caused him to make some of the decisions he chose to make. It ended well and everything is good between us. Now it's your turn to face your root problem so you can continue your journey of being the best version of yourself.

III

Insecurities & Pain

Now this is one of the hardest topics for us men to talk about. You know us "men" are secure about everything right? Well, a real man will tell you otherwise because no matter where you are from, your race, background, shape, or size we all have had insecurities as a boy growing up. The same way how we love to tell the women "you all are so insecure" well guess what ladies, so are we. The difference is we are too prideful to admit it because society tells us men are not supposed to be insecure. We are supposed to be tough, emotionless, loud, fearless and walk around with our chest out. Well you might as well throw that narrative out because that is completely false. It is also a part of the problem as to why some men are the way they are today.

Allow me to share some of my stories and insecurities so you can have a better insight on what I am talking about. Growing up my father was absent from the household. He was not absent from my life, but he was not always there as well. Therefore, growing up one of my insecurities was becoming a man and doing manly deeds such as changing the tire on a car, cutting grass, providing for an entire family, or just how to approach situations from a man's perspective. For those that grew up with a father that does not mean he will teach you all of the right things. However, you have a better chance than someone without a male in the household. Now I am pretty sure it sounds easy to say just go be a man right? Well ladies look at it from this perspective: if you tell a young lady who has never worn makeup before to go put make up on her face, she will not know how to do it correctly. She will do it the way that she believes makeup should be put on instead of the correct way because she had no example to emulate. It is the same concept with being a man, you cannot simply tell a boy how to be a man. We need guidance, instructions and visualization on how to do it the right way.

My insecurity with becoming a man also affected how I chose to deal with women and relationships. There were a lot of things that I did not know. Questions were constantly flowing through my mind: how do you approach a girl? How do you treat them? What do they like? How on earth do you get a girl to like you? When I started attending high school, I was always a decent looking guy but I was not the ladies first pick. The problem was the fact that I was shorter than a majority of my peers, including girls! According to the doctor, I was physically a "late bloomer".

Just to paint a more vivid picture, not only was I shorter than everyone but I was scrawny from genetics and wore braces because my teeth were horrific. There was not enough space in my mouth for my teeth to grow properly. So, not only did I lack the physical appearance but I had no idea on how to approach or treat a woman. Of course, I asked my mom for advice on the different questions that I did not know about girls. I decided to put my mom's advice to the test. I would buy my crush or girlfriend's flowers, candy, send them sweet good morning texts, write letters, the whole shebang. Now, they did like those things but they did not value them. What high school girls valued more was the most popular guy, the class clowns, the best dressed, the guy with the money or the star athletes. Does this sound familiar to anyone? Because this is not just a high school thing, as adults our value system can sometimes become distorted.

One of the things that people have to realize is that there is a difference between what we value versus what we prefer. Your values impact your preferences. Once you began to allow your preferences to dictate your values, your judgement can become cloudy. I am speaking to men specifically in the next few sentences. Men there is a difference between VALUING a big butt as opposed to that being your preferred figure in a woman. As men we have to stop valuing things that do not matter. Stop putting so much value into her wearing real or fake hair. Stop putting so much value in what shade of skin tone she is. Stop putting so much value into what she can do in the bedroom. Instead, value her character, her morals, her beliefs, her vision, her heart and most importantly her foundation. The same applies to women: stop putting so much value into a man's pocket, or what kind of car he drives. None of it matters if he does not treat you well or if his character and morals aren't good. An individual's foundation is what we all need to value.

Now back to my insecurities, I did play basketball throughout high school but again my appearance overshadowed that. The girlfriends or the girls that I would crush over would chase one of those type of guys that I previously stated. I was taught to be nice and a gentleman, but girls wouldn't take me serious because I was not that star athlete, class clown, or most popular guy. I began to feel insecure about getting a girlfriend or dealing with women period. From a male's perspective I already lacked the knowledge of a man, the physical appearance and now all the women want the type of guy that I was not. I began to ask myself why am I not good enough? Why do girls not take me serious? Am I ugly? Was I too short? I would ask a million questions as to why girls would not want me or take me serious. One day I got sick of being taken for granted when I would do nice things for women and that insecurity eventually turned into my pain. I began to hurt other people because as you know "hurt people, hurts others". I was truly hurt because although no one took me seriously, I could not handle girls taking advantage of me when I did nothing to deserve that. Now although I was hurting people, my intentions were never set out to purposely hurt them. I had put a wall up to prevent any further pain coming my way. I began to care more about my feelings as oppose to others, especially if I felt like I could get hurt in the process. I started becoming a different person, which was an a-hole. I started making selfish decisions that only concerned my feelings instead of others because I refused to get hurt again. Toward the end of my years in high school I developed the reputation of the a-hole. I had not one care about it because I was numb from my insecurities and the pain of people mistreating me.

Fast forward to college, I started to grow into my own. I had a growth spurt going from my freshman year in high school 4'11" to my freshman year in college 5'11". My braces had been removed for 2 years now but again I'm still a late bloomer so although I'm taller, I still have a baby face with no facial hair and the body of a freshman in high school at 145 lbs. I am playing basketball in college being around teammates and other students who are grown men with muscles, facial hair, and deep voices while I still sound like a kid in high school. As time goes by in college this wall becomes thicker and all the pressure of my pain and insecurities builds up because I chose not to tell anyone. I mean who could I tell? My friends would laugh at me and I was too embarrassed to tell my mother because I felt like she would not understand from a male's perspective. Therefore, I continued to let all of those negative emotions build up instead. As my college year goes by I am still thinking about myself, until I met a young woman that I actually began to like. I started to slowly allow my wall to come down and decided to give relationships a chance again. As the school year continued things were going well and I felt like I had fallen in love, well not true love but my definition of love at the time. The end of the year nears and she decided to break up with me for another guy. Not because I cheated, not because I mistreated her, not because things were getting bad but simply because she had eyes for another man. I then noticed a pattern, the majority of the women I crushed over began to like guys that were manlier physically. This turned into a new insecurity for me. At this point in my early college years I have two insecurities that began to build up over the years which was becoming a man and my relationship with women.

Now here comes my new and third insecurity creeping into my life, which was my scrawny body. The little bit of heart I had given to her went out the window. I automatically put the wall back up and started to hurt people again because I was torn. I sat in my room and cried for a week, lost sleep, and did not eat. It was not just the fact of breaking up but I was losing a best friend. This was someone that I spent so much time with - someone I shared my emotions and secrets with, all to be left for a more "manly" guy. I began to become so insecure about my body that I hated skinny jokes. I hated any comments about my size. Now I never lost sleep or cried over this insecurity but I hid it with a smile. I felt as though that was the cause of many of my problems. I believed that if I were manlier, people would take me serious and girls would want me.

I hated being skinny so much that I begin to get tattoos. During this time, getting tattoos was popular because Wiz Khalifa, Chris brown and other celebrities were making tattoos the new wave. Everyone was getting tattoos all over their bodies, so the timing was perfect for me. It seemed as though I was following the wave of tattoos but in actuality I was masking the insecurities of my body. The reason for me getting so many tattoos was because I was self-conscious about my body. My mindset at that time was the more tattoos that I get, the more it would distract people from my body size and more towards the tattoos. I never told anyone this secret so you all are the first that I am revealing this but the one thing that I learned about being self-conscious about my body is there is ABSOLUTELY NOTHING with my body. What I realized is, it's the rejection that bothered me, not so much my body. I've been rejected based on my body by women, sports, even a social life. As I stated growing up playing basketball my entire life, coaches would pass up on me or wouldn't give me an opportunity because of my size. Again nothing was wrong with my body but when you constantly get rejected for one thing, you began to question it. Most of our insecurities come from rejection and not even the thing we dislike about ourselves in the first place. There is not one tattoo on my body that I got from pleasure, it was all from pain due to a situation. I even thought about removing them but the tattoos I chose to put on my body are things that made me happy to balance out that pain I felt about my body or a situation I was dealing with. It was just something about the pain of needle taking away the pain of what I was going through. To give you a different perspective as to why I got tattoos, think about this. If I took my shirt off, what would be the first thing you would say? Would it be "Wow you are skinny or wow you have a lot of tattoos"? Exactly, 95% of the time the reaction would probably be that I have a lot of tattoos. This took the focus off my body and directed it towards the tattoos that I have. I thought about removing my tattoos once I became comfortable with my body but decided to keep them because they tell a story. Not only do they tell a story but all of my tattoos have a positive message that pertains to my life. I also decided to keep my tattoos because I also want people to understand you don't need a clean cut image to be a good person. A great person has nothing to do with physical appearance but 100% inner beauty.

I compare this to the similarity of when some women cut their hair after experiencing something dramatic. They cannot control what occurred but they can control how changing their appearance via a haircut makes them feel. Well, tattoos was my haircut and it made me feel good, at least temporarily. You see, not only as men but people as a whole, we mask our insecurities with different things such as cars, designer clothes, makeup, and other material things. My mask just happened to be tattoos. The problem is that in order for us to remain "fake" happy we have to continue to feed our insecurities. What we do not realize is that we are not fixing the problem but making it worse by masking it. Its equivalent to putting a Band-Aid over a cut that needs stitches.

After dealing with that last woman, I was so hurt that I decided to build my wall back up but even thicker than before. This way, no one was able to reach the real me. I was so afraid of being vulnerable and getting hurt that I began to hurt women at an alarming rate. I did not care about their feelings and did whatever I wanted to do. I was sleeping with women, going about my business, playing mind games and said whatever I felt regardless if it hurt their feelings or not. The ones I did begin to like I would push them away before they could break my wall. At any point where I felt some type of feelings gaining towards the woman, I would sabotage the relationship so she can leave. I could not take any more pain of my past. In actuality, I was hurting all of these women creating a giant cycle of pain and not even realizing it. Now that they were hurt, they began to hurt other people as well. The whole ordeal becomes a vicious cycle of hurt people, hurting other people.

At the time I had no care in the world because I was only protecting my feelings. My mentality was either her feelings or mine, which I chose mine every single time. That behavior went on for so long that it became habitual. Not only was I hurting others but I was digging myself further into a hole with my own insecurities. As my college years continued I met another young woman with same the intentions, sex and be friends or not talk at all. Being in a committed relationship still was not an option at this point because I was too fearful of the same cycle happening to me. This time it was different as I began to like who she was as a person. She was different, her mentality attracted me, how she carried herself was different and the respect she demanded would not allow me to treat her the way that I wanted to. As time went on we began to get to know each other but we also experienced many problems. Most of the problems were my fault due to the insecurities and pain I had not yet dealt with. You see, because I chose not to fix my insecurities and release them at an early age it became a huge roadblock for me. I realized that an individual can only accept as much love as they can give. Because I was still insecure and hurting, I was not giving out any love. When I did want to receive the love that this woman tried to give, I could not because the walls that I had built would not allow me to. I now understand that if I chose to work on my insecurities I would have been able to receive the love I always wanted. Notice I said MY love because true love is unlimited. We all have our own idea of love and through that we have certain expectations of how things should be.

When those expectations are not met, there will be problems within the relationship. When we make up our own definition of love, outside of God's love, it will fail every single time.

The woman that I was seeing, I made her fight to break down my wall of insecurities. By the time she almost reached the core of who I really was, she had no strength left in her to continue on. My wall of insecurities and pain was so thick that had I drained someone that I loved – (again, by my definition) because I did not deal with my issues earlier. Granted, she had insecurities and pain she had not dealt with that I fought through as well, but nonetheless my insecurities played a major role in the destruction of our relationship. Had I given all of that over to God, I would not have created such heartache to those individuals who cared about me. You should never want to be in a situation where you lose your potential wife, friends or anyone in general that you love because you have not unpacked that luggage. This is why I am sharing this so that you can avoid what I have endured and the damage that I have caused to others.

We must deal with our insecurities, our pain and our secrets as soon as possible. Give them to God so he can use you to turn it into good. Parents make sure you have daily or weekly talks with your children to help them deal with those things in life that does not give them peace. Pay special attention to our young males because one of their biggest issues will be communication. As males, we were taught not to cry, be tough all the time, and to suck up our emotions because we will be okay. Do you know the dangers of what that leads to? It leads to years of bottled up emotions because society tells us men only express toughness. In reality, it is actually weakness if a man cannot express how he truly feels. Men we have to do better with teaching our young men this concept so that they will not have years of pent up emotions. Because I did not communicate for many years in my previous relationships, when I finally experienced one that I wanted to be in I was lost in the communication department. This was a major factor in the destruction of my relationships. This added to another fear that I have to this day of being a good boyfriend or good husband. I had allowed my insecurities to go unresolved for such a long time that other insecurities started to develop from the ones that I already had. It is almost as if they started to give birth to other fears. I have now made the choice to release them to God and work on self-love. From that point on, he helped me to heal so that I could share my story. Hopefully, this will prevent someone from making the same mistakes that I made. It does not matter what age you are. My point is, if you are alive to read this then it is not too late for you either. Start today and make the choice to be better not only for yourself but to teach others so that they do not have to experience what we went through.

"The pain that you have been feeling can't compare to the joy that is coming" - Romans 8:18

IV

Where does understanding dwell?

We live in a society that seems to get worse and worse by the day. The world always had its rough times but it seems like this world will never get better. Our country seems divided fighting amongst ourselves, our neighborhoods seem divided, even our own households in many places.

Someone asked me a question recently and said, "How do you feel about the president?" I asked, "what do you mean how do I feel about him?" Now I know what they were asking but I preferred a more specific question, so I can give a specific answer instead of a broad one. Although a lot of people may disagree with how the president handles certain situations, I think the problems are so much bigger than the president and our problems existed way before the president got here. What I mean is, we all come from so many different places, cultures, backgrounds, experiences, and walks through life. The same thing that makes it beautiful is the same reason why things have become so ugly. The biggest issues I believe we have in this country are Lack of Communication, Lack of Understanding, and Lack of Empathy.

Lack of Communication

The fact that we come from all different places in this world, as well as our different upbringings, means we all communicate in many different ways." We speak differently, we have different accents, we use different signs, symbols, and gestures. We all have a different sense of humor, we cry at different things but ultimately the way everyone communicates is endlessly different.

An example of this would be someone who grew up in a wealthy background and someone who grew up in a poverty-stricken environment. Now, if you have two individuals who grew up in those environments and the person from the wealthy background has never been in an area that is poverty-stricken, something small such as language could be a problem. From personal experience, many people who "speak proper" have a hard time understanding someone who speaks a lot of slang, not to mention people who have accents depending on where they are from. Now because these two individuals are from different places, there is a language barrier in which neither party can understand each other.

Let's take it to a larger scale and tackle the elephant in the room with problems we are all facing now. I think racism is still a present problem in America whether people want to admit it or not. I don't mean from a perspective of white and black but all races, all across the board. Let's take the Colin Kaepernick story, for example. A lot of people from many different places have their own opinion on this matter. Some people are angry he chose to do it on that platform, some people are upset with the injustice that people of color in this country experience. Many people felt like he disrespected the flag and some people felt like he made the correct decision with peaceful protest. However you feel about the matter, we all have a right to our opinion whether some disagree or respect what we have to say. Needless to say Colin Kaepernick decision to kneel was his form of communication to the world on how he felt about the state we are currently experiencing in this country.

Understanding

Two big issues remain after lack of communication: lack of understanding and lack of empathy. People feel so strongly about their opinion that the way they are communicating is in a negative manner. Cursing, screaming, calling names, and pointing the finger is not a positive way of communication and what that does is cause people to be defensive, protecting themselves and their feelings by any means necessary. The problem is no one wants to meet in the middle and communicate the right way, even if they agree to disagree. People are so caught up in themselves and their opinions that they just want to shove their opinion down the other person's throat. This eventually causes the other person to have "deaf ears" to the communication process.

Now, because we all come from different walks of life, when you are trying to communicate, you must understand who you are talking to and how they may be receptive to your information. A lot of people are more receptive to a softer tone of voice and some are more receptive to an aggressive, argumentative way of communicating. It definitely matters who you are communicating with. Once you come to an agreement on how you will communicate, that is when understanding takes place among people. Although I think all three steps – communication, understanding, and empathy – are important, I personally think understanding is the most important one. Let's take a more realistic approach such as a racist older white male and a young black male. Both have a different skin color, both come from different backgrounds, both experience an age gap from the other person, and both feel strongly about their opinion towards the other. Now, the first thing that happens when these two men meet is probably tension, awkwardness and even hatred for each other because the older white male doesn't like black people and the black male doesn't like white people. These two will automatically become defensive, so they will need to find some "middle ground" for their communication process or communication agreement to even sit down and have a conversation. Once that has happened and Understanding has introduced itself to the table, both must be mature enough to listen to what the other person has to say.

Empathy

When we listen, we must actually listen to understand and not listen just to respond. What a lot of people do is once the other person starts to talk, we already know what we want to say and we hold on to that until the other person is finished, not even trying to understand what the other person is saying. Say for example the white male and the black male meet at the table. I'm sure both parties have questions as to why they have certain feelings towards each other. They both may have unanswered questions such as "why don't you like me? What did I do to you?" The questions that needs to be asked are "who, what, when, where, why, and how". The questions can be formulated on your own but as long as you cover the who, what, when, where, why, and how, I promise you will get the answers you are looking for.

The biggest difference between Understanding and empathy is when you are trying to empathize for someone, your goal is to understand from an emotional stand point. It is stepping out of our shoes and putting someone else's shoes for the sole purpose of understanding emotionally. We have no idea what a person has experienced, which is why it is very important to try to understand the other person even if you don't like or agree with how they feel or what they say. What if the white male grew up in a home where all he was told was that "black people are evil" and "black people are the devil"? Although he will grow up to have his own opinion one day, is he really at fault if he has been told these things about black people all of his life? This is not to justify racism but this discussion is coming from a place of understanding and empathizing. He really didn't grow up with a choice because his parents put hate in him for black people since birth. He didn't have a fair chance at formulating his own opinion.

As for the black male, what if he has been picked on and beaten up by white people all his life and the majority of white people have said nasty things to him. His perception will be negative towards all white people based on his experience. Now does that justify to judge all white people based on his experience? No because all white people aren't the same. Once these two express how they feel and say, "Hey, although you experienced that, all black people are not the same and all white people are not the same," then they can move forward. Of course it's easier said than done because there are people who are not willing to even get that far in conversation, but for the people that are willing, this is how you try to get to a place of empathy. If both parties actually ask the right questions, with the other person's point of view or experience, that's where the empathy comes in.

    The hardest part of empathy is putting your feelings on hold and putting the other person's feelings into your heart. You have to disregard your feelings that you care so much about for five seconds just to wear someone else's feelings. You have to remove your ego and put yourself in their shoes, live through their eyes, and see life from their perspective. I think this is the most difficult step because it is very challenging to put yourself in someone else's shoes if you didn't have the same experiences they had.

    Just as it is important to communicate, understand and empathize on big issues, it is important to do it with smaller issues as well. Although I used very uncomfortable but real subjects from today's society, you can start applying these three things to your personal relationships with family members, friends, or even your partner. I believe the reason why so many relationships go bad is because of lack of communication. I never really understood what that meant because communication seemed so easy until I got older and realized how deep communication is. We all go through problems in our relationships and although communication is a big reason why they fail, we don't realize understanding and empathy is included in communicating.

I personally have been in a situation where I said something to my girlfriend that didn't sit well with her. At the time, I felt what I said wasn't worth her being hurt over so in a sense, I brushed it off. When my girlfriend presented how she was feeling because of what I said, I stated I was sorry – but also proceeded to say that I don't think it was worth being mad over. Now, that approach was completely wrong because although we came to a place of communication, I lacked true understanding of how she felt in which caused me to have no empathy for how she felt. I disregarded her feelings and was caught up in my own egotistic behavior of how I thought she should have felt instead of how she truly felt. If I would have come to the table with full understanding of how she felt, then I would have displayed empathy. I wouldn't have disregarded her feelings and made them seem of no importance.

This is where many of us go wrong because we get through the communication phase but we don't try to fully understand our partners because we are too caught up in our own feelings which adds another issue. Sometimes, we only try to understand the person as much as WE want instead of as much as THEY want. We cannot get to a place of empathy if we don't get past the understanding phase. Now granted, there will be times where you just don't fully understand how someone feels but if you care about your partner or anyone you have a serious relationship with, you won't do it again. At some point in life you will understand how your partner felt, even if its months or years down the line. If we want better relationships all across the board, we must follow the three phases. Communication is the first step, Understanding is the most important step, and Empathy is the hardest step. I promise if we try our best and put our egos to the side, we are one step closer to making a positive impact on the world.

V

Your foundation (Relationships)

Now before we start this chapter, I just want to point out that I AM NOT A MARRIAGE OR RELATIONSHIP EXPERT but I have experienced being in numerous relationships and I can definitely give some insight on where I went wrong and where most people make the same mistake without even noticing. As I stated, I've been in numerous relationships from high school up until now. Some relationships were amazing and some were not so well but nonetheless they all ended whether on good or bad terms. Now because I grew up in a single parent household, I had no idea of how a relationship was supposed to go which was one of my insecurities. So every relationship I was in was trial and error and I only acted out how I thought a relationship should go based on observation, TV shows, or word of mouth. Now here is mistake number one that most people make with relationships. We develop our own idea of what we think a relationship is or should be. If you go ask 10 random people what a relationship is, I can bet you there will be some different answers because we define it to our standards. Well guess what? I too made that same exact mistake with all of my relationships. From the very moment I started dating I only had the few examples of what I thought a relationship was. Based on TV shows and movies, things were supposed to be close to perfect. Yes I knew we wouldn't always be happy and we would disagree a few times but I figured it was about giving gifts, buying her favorite candy, movie dates, and sex right? Well that relationship had some good moments but it ended. It ended because although I thought I knew that person, we didn't take our time. Now granted I was still a teenager so relationships at that time wasn't that deep because I didn't know the in depth things about it yet. Movies and Tv shows don't teach you that because in movies you run into a stranger at the grocery, you bump into them and knock the groceries out her hand, help her pick it up, apologize then get wide eyed and go with the "love at first sight theme". You then go on a few dates, start liking each other, go through some dramatic scene in the movie where the women or man stop talking, then towards the end of the movie they run towards each other in the rain, kiss , fall in love, have a family and happy ending. Now I'm not saying those things don't happen but for majority people it doesn't happen that way because relationships are not that simple. To be honest, I wish they were that simple but once I realized how serious relationships are I started took it more serious. It's not that I didn't take relationships as a joke but I didn't take it as serious as I do now because I understand how much responsibility it is and what is really at stake. Now mistake number two I would make is jumping from girl to girl or relationship to relationship. The reasons why I made those choices was because 1. I felt like I learned my mistakes from the last relationship so if I don't make that same mistake, the next relationship would be successful. Reason number 2. Is I just enjoyed being in a relationship that much and last reason was to forget about the last relationship I just got out of. Once I got out of a relationship I would want to forget about the last girlfriend so I would entertain or date someone else. The problem with jumping from girl to girl was I was only hurting myself and not even realizing it. What I was doing and what many people do is carry the baggage from the last relationship into the next one without even unloading all or at least some of it. So when you date back to back and are in your 4th relationship, you still have the baggage from your 1st to 3rd relationship and put weight on the 4th one. In total I've had 5 girlfriends in my entire life but most, if not all were back to back dealings with a woman. My first relationship caused me to have fear of getting close, my second one caused me to have trust issues, my third one caused me to have regret, and my fourth one caused me to have an insecurity. Now that I was going into my fifth relationship and I was hopping from woman to woman, I brought all of those things on one woman. Now imagine a woman trying to bare the weight of fear, trust issues, regret, and insecurity along with all of her own problems? That is a lot for just one person to deal with so imagine whatever she brought into our relationship is double the weight of us trying to not only learn each other but unpack our baggage because we chose not to fix it first. See a lot of us have that issue of jumping from person to person not realizing you are effecting not only yourself but the other person as well. You both go into the relationship as broken people looking for that void of hurt to be filled but the reality is two broken people cannot love each other unless you fix yourself up first. The solution to that is find finding self-love before you can give yourself to someone. In between these times that you break up you need to take a break to work on yourself, appreciate some me time, and unload some of that hurt and baggage from your last relationship. Trust me it will stop you from getting into a relationship that you have no business getting into just cause you were vulnerable or use that person as a rebound.

    Mistake number three that most of us make is creating our own definition of love. Now although I dated some of my girlfriends for the wrong reasons I did end up liking every single one of those women and even fell in love with two of them to my standards. Notice I said to "MY" standards because the problem majority us do is develop our own idea of what love is. Many of us have never experienced true love because we come up with our own definition. I call this subject "The idea of love" which is similar to the idea of what we think a relationship should be. I know women who personally think love is getting abused physically and emotionally. Their excuse would be "I know he hits me and curses me out but he only does that because he loves me and wants the best for me." That was her idea of love because when she was growing up she saw people being mistreated with the word "love" attached to it and in her mind that was love. For the guys, you see some consistently cheat and tell their girlfriends "I love you and the sex didn't mean nothing it was just physical." That was his idea of love because of his upbringing and seeing his father do it so understand because a lot of us haven't experienced true love, we develop our own ideas of what we think love should be. Even If it isn't abusive we could think it should be you spend all your time together, going on vacations 24/7, showering each other with gifts, or taking cute pictures and posting them on social media. When you develop your own ideas of love the relationship won't last because we often have unrealistic expectations and when those expectations aren't met you get disappointed but in reality it is your fault for replacing God's definition of love with your own. There is only one true love which is God's love and the minute you replace it with your own "idea of love" or the world's definition of love, you are setting yourself up for failure. I have done this twice and both times I was in love by my standard and when things didn't go how I expected it caused traumatic heart breaks. Once I understood what I did by replacing God's love with my own, I took responsibility for myself and decided to never define love by my standards but only God's standards. "4 Love is patient, love is kind. It does not envy, it does not boast, it is not proud. 5 It does not dishonor others, it is not self-seeking, it is not easily angered, it keeps no record of wrongs.6 Love does not delight in evil but rejoices with the truth. 7 It always protects, always trusts, always hopes, always perseveres.

8 Love never fails." I know we hear that often and it might be cliché but the more you understand the definition the more it will make sense because it didn't fully make sense to me at first but now I have a deeper understanding of what love is. Never forget this and read it to make sure your idea of love matches with God's love or it will fail trust me. Now the most important question is how do I find love? Well In order to find true love you must seek God first. For years I would hear seek God and I would hear the definition of Love but it still didn't click in my mind from a place of understanding. One day in my process of getting closer to God, I stumbled upon a video by TD Jakes. I

don't remember what exactly what the video was about but what I do know is that the video connected the dots and everything made perfect sense to me from there on out.

How many of us have chosen to date someone because they looked good? Or because they had money? Or because the sex was so good you fell into a relationship on accident? Well I myself am very guilty of this without a doubt. When I chose to get in a relationship with all of those women, I did like all of their personality but I also dated them for other reasons. Some I dated because the sex was good, some was because I knew we would look good together physically, and some because they were popular and no one had the chance to date them. From the moment we began to date, our foundation was wrong and that is probably the most important mistake that most of us make. We date the person for the wrong reason and the foundation on which you started with is weak. Let me put it into a different perspective. If a woman seeks a man for his money, his physical appearance, his sex or any of those things then that is the foundation in which she chooses to build her relationship on. The same thing goes for a man who seeks a woman for her physical appearance, her sex, her career, or anything of the sort. Let me ask you a question. If the foundation of your relationship is based upon sex what happens when it gets boring? If it is appearance, what happens when you start to age? If it is for money, what happens if they go broke? Do you see where I am going with this? All of those things come and go or someone else out there has more and if that's the foundation that holds your relationship together, what happens when that is gone? Exactly, the relationship is gone and it was never built on a strong foundation to begin with. What is a good foundation for an everlasting relationship? The simple answer is God and love. This is the moment in my life where the dots connected and everything made sense about love, relationships, and your foundation. When you seek God, what you are doing is finding yourself and in between you finding your true self, you are developing an intimate relationship with God which leads to a million different avenues. See when you seek an intimate relationship with God you are learning how to love, you are learning patience, you are learning how to be faithful, you are learning how to be kind, what you are doing is learning how to love and once you learn those things with God, you learn how to love your partner, be patient with your partner, learn how to be faithful and kind to your partner because God taught you those qualities in the relationship you were seeking with the God. Everything you learn when you are developing a relationship with God is what you do to your partner and that becomes your foundation to a strong relationship. If you wouldn't do it to God don't do it to your partner and what you do to God is what you do to your partner. If you wouldn't disrespect God or curse God don't curse your partner or disrespect your partner because marriage is under God. You love your wife the way you love God, you are faithful to your wife the way you are to God and so forth. I heard a talk from a famous public speaker by the name of Tony Gaskins and a quote stuck with me that said a weak foundation is like building a mansion on sand. I'm sure you can put two and two together of how that house will end up. Tony Gaskins and his wife are completely opposites with the exceptions of their foundation which says a lot. No matter what you like, where you are from or what you look like, if you have a strong foundation of God and God has assigned that person to your life then the relationship will work. Lay down your foundation, seek God first, fall in love with yourself and God will order your steps from there.

VI
Purpose Filled

What is your purpose in life? Have you ever reflected on the reason you are here? What on earth am I supposed to be doing for the rest of my life? Whatever it is we all are meant to serve other people to do great and amazing things. We all have gifts, desires and things we want to accomplish. There are many people out there who feel lost and hopeless because they feel as though they serve no purpose. They feel as though they are just living, taking up space and have no idea what direction to go. A lot of times we miss out on our purpose because we are distracted by the world and such things as money, relationships, partying, fear, worrying or whatever the case may be. There is nothing wrong with those things but there is a time and place for everything. Where we continue to mess up is when we want to do things OUR way, thinking we have all the answers to life but we don't. God has a plan and a path for all of us but we have to make the right choices and stay on the path to find our purpose. I find that our society is so money hungry or ego driven that we are willing to work jobs we hate, go against morals, and lose ourselves in the process just to have a lot of money or just to have things our way. Although money does solve many problems, the saying "more money more problems" isn't just a phrase but very true. Many people have no idea what they are getting themselves into by allowing the wrong things to guide them through life. People watch entertainers on television with a lot of money, thinking all their problems are solved and they are living wonderful lives, not realizing many of them are depressed and broken because of the problems money brought them. A lot of entertainers have millions of dollars but have no peace whatsoever. I'm not saying money isn't important but what does it profit a man, if he gains the whole world, and lose his own soul? You will live a life putting so much into something that you can't even take with you when you die. Is that what you want your legacy to be? Someone with a lot of money who died? Don't chase the money, don't chase love, or the material things. We all love those things but understand what I mean when I say, don't chase those things. Don't make that the number one priority in your life to where you miss out on your purpose. I grew up with the understanding that men would do anything to impress women, so they would chase after them constantly. Then I heard the saying, if you chase the money, the women will follow. Do you want to live a life where you place so much value into those things that when you lose it, you feel as though you have nothing to live for? Everything you want or desire is on the other side of your PURPOSE. "But seek ye first the kingdom of God and his righteousness, and all these things will be added to you". What that means is seek the lord with all your heart, allow him to order your footsteps into your purpose and EVERYTHING you need will be added unto you. "Look at the birds of the air: they neither sow nor reap nor gather into barns, and yet your heavenly Father feeds them. Are you not of more value than they?" You see we focus on trying to get five different things all at the same time which stresses us out, but we won't have to worry about a job, money, or a home because if we focus on one thing which is seeking the lord and our purpose, everything else will fall into place. Our purpose will give us so much fulfillment because we are not only doing something we love, but we are also helping millions of people in the process and not even realizing it. I always thought my purpose would be dribbling a basketball on someone's court. I've been playing basketball as long as I can remember all the way up to college level. I was never NBA talent but I was a pretty good player. I wondered what would be my purpose because I just knew God gave me that gift to play basketball. As time went by and I developed a new love for writing, things began to make a lot more sense. Basketball was my purpose for that time but it was a platform that gave me the opportunity to meet certain people and also to mold me into my purpose for writing as well as use that experience to help other people. I don't think I would have impacted as many people as I did playing basketball as oppose to writing blogs and writing this book. Basketball will always be something I love and I'm sure it was a part of the plan but I honestly get more fulfillment while impacting the world and change peoples' lives of all ages through my writings. I have never been motivated by money or allowed money to be my driving force to make a decision. I've always wanted to serve my purpose to help others first because I knew I would be genuinely happy in that way. For those who don't know their purpose yet, I know how it feels because I use to ask myself that question.

Ever wake up and feel like you are at a standstill? Like things aren't moving fast enough and you're stuck in a hard place where you can't see the light at the end of the tunnel? I think we all have felt like we were in situations where things were not going to get better or we felt like things were not moving fast enough but GOD's timing is always perfect. We live in such a fast pace society that we don't appreciate anything that takes time to develop. Think about it like this, if God gave you a million dollars every month how fast would you spend the money? 1. I'm sure most would because you knew you would be getting it right back and 2. You didn't work for it so you wouldn't appreciate it as much. It's not about getting the money every month, it's about the timing of the blessing and are you prepared for it. Whether we sit around waiting for a job, car, house, or even a relationship, we don't have some of these things because God wants us to be ready for them. It is the exact same thing for our purpose. As I asked myself what my purpose is and why am I not serving it, the reality was, I just wasn't ready for my ultimate purpose. We serve small purposes and go through our daily routine of life that molds us so we can be prepared and ready for our ultimate purpose so that we can appreciate it in its' ENTIRETY. With great power comes great responsibility so when given our purpose, we must be prepared and responsible with that blessing. Are you doing the necessary things to prepare yourself for great responsibility? Are you working on yourself? Are you working on your weaknesses? Are you praying daily? Are you being obedient? Are you putting in effort? And one of the most important things, are you planting your seed?

I never fully understood the saying, plant your seed and get ready for a seasonal change. I understood on the surface but just not in depth of what it meant. It sounds so cliché but once I gained understanding, it became clear. This fast paced society we live in, we want things right now without doing long consist work for it. Instant gratification has set the standard for so many things that it has caused us to be impatient in our process. Most things that are worth having take a while to get and a lot of hard work to keep, so when you hear the phrase "planting your seeds" that is exactly what it means. Putting in a lot of hard work but not being able to see the results as quickly as we would like. It is similar to attending school, we put in a lot of work daily but won't see the reward until the end of the semester and our final grade. It is the exact same thing as our purpose because in order for us to see results we have to be willing to put in hours of work and not expect instant gratification. Just as it takes an entire season for a plant to become beautiful and blossom, it takes an entire season for our purpose to become fulfilled but the question in the meantime is are you planting your seed? Are you putting in hours of work knowing you won't see any results until the seasons change? Are you being consistent? Are you giving maximum effort? Are you taking this serious? Once I asked those questions it changed my perception on everything and I quickly threw away the instant gratification desire. My problem was giving up when I didn't see results as quickly I wanted to because I was so use to getting things so fast I became naturally impatient. Once I began to ponder on the concept of seasonal changes and planting seeds, I started to develop a desire for patience and instead of focusing on the present, I focused on the finish line and embraced the long process. One question I asked all my life was "what do you want to be when you grow up?" Or "what career do you want to pursue?" I had many ideas I would consider doing but I never truly knew what I wanted to do 100%. All I knew was, I wanted to serve my purpose whatever it was, so I focused on that. I stopped comparing my life to my fellow peers. Yes some people motivated me to do better by doing amazing things but I've learned everyone's life is different, their life is for them and my life is for me. Once I realized what I was supposed to be doing, I no longer worried about the pain of the process or the amount of time I was putting in because I embraced it. See we can't have the good without the bad in the process of planting our seed so it is better to embrace it while focusing on the lessons until the season changes. That is with anything in life because if you are preparing for a relationship you plant your seed by being the best version of yourself by working hard on yourself so when that person comes you are ready. That job you have been wanting, you must work hard and practice for it so when it is presented, it will be easy. If you are planning to work out to gain or lose weight, you will not see results the first week but if you continue to keep working on it and focus less on the pain and more on the finish product, you will get there. Are you preparing for your season? Are you planting your seeds so when it comes, you are fully prepared? Sometimes we make things harder than what they are because we stand in our own way looking for different ways to get there faster in when actuality the seeds are in our hand the entire time. Although you may not know your purpose, you can figure out your gifts that you are aware of in the meantime. I encourage you to grab a piece of paper and write down all the things you passionate about, all the gifts or things you are good at, and write down the careers that many people suggested you would be good at. I didn't realize I could write until I was 20 years old and at the age of 26 is when I took it serious because I realized everything I wrote down aligned with writing. It matched with my personality, I was helping people, and many people would give suggestions to write a book which was confirmation for me so the decision was easy. Before I realized my gift I felt as though I was like everyone else and that is something I feel we all struggle with because we don't think the small things are gifts as well. Being funny, relatable, witty, holding an interesting conversation for a long time, making people smile, understanding, giving advice, all those are gifts but because we feel as though we aren't the best at it or because we don't stand out, those aren't gifts. In order to reach your purpose you must use your small gifts as a supporting cast because they are just as important. Imagine you are cooking a giant thanksgiving dinner for your family in which you have turkey, macaroni and cheese, dressing, collard greens, sweet potatoes and dinner rolls. All of those things are the finished product but what is also important is the seasoning and spices in each and every one of those dishes. Your big gifts are the finished product such as the thanksgiving food but your small and supporting gifts such as the seasonings are what makes the food unique. Many people can make the entire dinner but what sets people apart is the small details within the food. Focus on your small details as well because they are overlooked, focus on the foundation of your gifts to reach the bigger purpose.

We don't have all the answers to life, so humble yourself, take one day at a time and all the bad things you go through, those are the times that are molding you for your purpose! Whatever your purpose is, it's meant to help others because OUR purpose is so much bigger than us, no matter what, don't give up and don't let anyone tell you otherwise. Stay focused on the goal ahead and have faith you will get there. If you get distracted catch yourself and get back on track. No one ever said the path would be easy, but it will be worth it. Now go tap into your purpose starting today and enjoy the journey to get there. Love & Positivity ♥□♥□♥□!

VII

Pain in your purpose (The Valley)

Often enough we go through tough times and wonder why we must endure the pain of life. We focus on "why me" so much that we miss the lesson. One thing we must remember there is PURPOSE IN OUR PAIN. By that I mean there is a reason why we go through tough times and pain. In order for us to grow and find ourselves, we must go through rough times. We don't go through times in vain but because there is a PURPOSE and a reason behind EVERYTHING IN LIFE. It may be because GOD is trying to get us to our purpose, it may be to learn a lesson, or because a bad decision we have made but for whatever reason there is a purpose, it is our job to find that purpose. Anytime you go through a rough patch in life remember all the other times you made it out and the lessons you learned along the way. Our greatest lessons come from tough times and it molds us to be the strong person we are today!!! In actuality we need rough times to remind us how strong we truly are and how we can overcome anything we set our mind to IF we just focus on the lesson and not the pain. Remember there is beauty in the struggle but we just have to remind ourselves to look for it. GOD never gives us more than we can handle but you have to stay positive. I didn't always believe that until God showed me the purpose in my pain.

It was the summer of 2011 and that was the first time I had my heart broken. I was dating a woman and to make a long story short, she broke up with me for someone else. I instantly went into a state of depression where I ended up crying, not eating, and sleeping more than usual for an entire week. That was the first time I hit a low point; I was always taught when you have nowhere else to run to, turn to God. I began praying heavily, reading the bible and even printing out bible scriptures and posting them on my wall. I prayed so much and so hard, that I heard God's voice for the first time. That was the closest I was to God at that point in my life and it was something I will never forget. Although I heard God's voice, I wanted everyone to understand my pain so I would write positive messages about my situation or a subject everyone could relate too. I would send it to all my friends and a few people would like my messages. In reality, it was a cry for help but I wasn't good at communicating, so I wrote my pain in messages hoping someone would sense I was hurting but it didn't work. However, it did help other people come to the realization that we were going through similar things and we weren't the only ones feeling that type of pain. As time went on I eventually healed, but I took a break from writing because I was focused on school and basketball.

Five years passed and there was a point in my life where I felt I hit rock bottom again. I hit another low point in my life but it was a lot worse. I was lost, confused and my life just felt like it was tearing apart in different directions. I lost my grandmother on December 29, 2016 from cancer and I remember that day like it was yesterday. I actually remember the days leading up to that because it was around Christmas and I was spending time with my son for the holidays. I received a call from my father saying that my grandmother went to the hospital and she was on the breathing machine. I wanted to break down but I held it together because I still wanted to enjoy my son for the remaining time I had left with him. As I was driving back on an 8 hour ride, I was speeding trying to get home before she passed away. My dad called me while I was on the road and I just stared at the phone, very nervous to pick it up because I didn't want to hear my grandmother left me while on the road. I ended up calling him back and he told me she is still on the breathing machine but wasn't responsive, I started driving faster because I wasn't too far from home. I got to the hospital and I was already aware the doctors couldn't do anything more for her. As I entered the room, I started to cry because I just wanted to say goodbye and tell her I love her one last time, I wanted her to say, "I love you too". The next day I was sleeping and my uncle woke me up to let me know my grandmother passed. At that point I didn't know how to feel because it was too surreal for my mind to wrap around. My second mom, one of my best friend's, someone who loved me with her entire heart, the woman who had a lot to do with raising me as well as introduced me to GOD was gone and I couldn't believe it was happening. I held up fine for a while because I tricked my mind into believing I was fine. My birthday rolled around three weeks later, my grandmother was always one of the first to call to tell me happy birthday. This year I had to accept I wasn't going to hear her voice on the other side of the phone. Although I had a great birthday that year, my grandmother was still on my mind as the day was ending. I texted my sister to tell her how I was feeling and she told me to pray. I went to pray, fell asleep and had one of the most vivid dreams I ever had in my life. I walked into a big party with family and friends dancing, eating, playing music and having a great time. I look over to my right and saw a woman in an all-white dress but was glowing really bright which turned out to be my grandmother. I went and gave her a hug but I realized I was the only one able to see her. We laughed, danced and just had a great time the entire party. As the party was ending I was heading towards the door and asked her if she was going home with me. She gave me a big smile and said "now you know I can't go with you baby." I asked her please can she come with me and she hops in the car for a ride. As I'm driving we are laughing and talking like the many times we use to do but after a few more minutes of driving, I looked over and she was gone. I woke up and began to cry because not only did I miss her but I felt like she was letting me know she was fine. As time went by I was fine emotionally because I remained positive and thought about how she would want me to live my life but towards the end of the year it really started to weigh in on me that she was gone and I'd never see her or hear her voice in this lifetime. I began to feel lost, sad, angry, confused and many other emotions mixed into giant ball. That's the first time I ever felt that many emotions at one time and I couldn't handle it. I begin to isolate myself from people, ignore phone calls, not eat as much, smoking weed, and drinking more. I stopped caring about life and just wanted to be happy again. I felt so lost I actually forgot how it felt to be genuinely happy which ate me up. In my darkest hours I begin to pray to God and asked him to restore my happiness. In between that time I would write long positive messages to my friends and my social media followers so it would at least brighten someone else's day since my life wasn't going good. They would enjoy my writings and would tell me how much it helped them in their current situations. After a while I felt as though God didn't hear my prayers so as time went by I began to ask myself, what am I here for? What is my purpose being on earth because I'm lost, confused, and felt like I was at a standstill, so what am I really here for? Instead of asking for happiness, I prayed for God to reveal my purpose but it was a selfish prayer because although it was for God to use me, my happiness was my first concern and I knew whatever God had planned for me would make me happy. Now I did genuinely want to fulfill God's purpose but I just put my happiness above all because I missed being happy and got tired of feeling so lost. As a few months went by I still felt like God wasn't listening to me and wasn't answering my prayers. I still believed in God but I felt like why aren't you helping me when I need you the most right now? In between that time I still continued to write long positive messages to my friends and random people on my social media not only to help but if figured the more positivity I put out, the more if would receive back which would at least make me feel better that I could brighten someone's day. Fast forward to May 18, 2017 I got into a bad car crash which resulted in my car being totaled. I was extremely thankful I didn't die and the very first thing I did when I got outside my car was thanked God. Although I was alive, I was in pain and began to think how am I going to work and still take care of the bills with no job? Well at that time I was living with my uncle and because I lost two jobs due to the accident, I had no income and I couldn't pay my portion of the bills. We were forced to move out and I end up moving with my aunt and a house full of younger cousins. Between the time last year which was 2016 and before I got into the car crash, I was still praying for happiness and my purpose. I was at a point where I had no job, no car and my money was running out. I was sleeping on the couch every night wondering how life could get any worse but reminded myself that I still had a roof over my head, food, clean clothes, and a family that truly loves me. While all of this is transpiring, I was still writing and sending my messages out to different people about many different subjects. Over that year my following grew bigger and people were suggesting all these ideas like I should write a blog, create a positivity app, write a book, and even become a public speaker. Now this was at least 50 plus people telling me I should do one of those things but I brushed it off because I was only spreading positivity because I enjoyed helping people get through rough times but I had zero interest in doing any of those things my followers suggested. So while I have no job, no car, and little money, I still prayed but I went back to a state of feeling low and lost. I could not understand why God was allowing these things to happen to me. Was it something I did? Am I reaping what I sowed? Are you trying to tell me something? God I need answers because I just don't understand why this is happening to me. I began to pray and ask God why can't I hear your voice? Why aren't you talking to me while I'm praying? Lord I just don't want to pray to you and you are not talking to me. I don't want this to be a one way conversation please answer me and let me know what is going on, please help me Father. Time continued to pass and I was sleeping a lot more because sleeping took me away from my reality of pain for a couple hours. I started to cry probably more than I ever had because I really didn't know what to do. Even though all this was taking place, I still continued to write my positive messages. Again my following grew and more people suggested blogs, books, speaking and apps. I brushed it off and said no I'm OK, I'm just doing this to help you all out but thank you for the suggestions. One day I ran into a great reading on praying and a relationship with God. The reading stated having an intimate relationship with God and not just about praying and going through the routines. I went from praying for my happiness, to praying for my purpose, to praying to hear God's voice, and my last and final prayer was an intimate relationship with God. I genuinely wanted to know God as my best friend, how he operates, who, what, why, when, where, and how from A to Z. I asked God for an intimate relationship and meant it wholeheartedly and things changed from that point on. I consistently prayed for an intimate relationship and that's when God began to talk to me in a variety of ways. The very first way I noticed is, he was using other people to speak to me. My friend sent me a random video on YouTube from TD Jakes called "Secretly Fighting" and that video was 1000% perfect for what I was going through at the time. If you are going through something similar or even if you aren't I encourage you to listen because that was the video that woke me up. After that prayer of asking for intimacy, God began talking to me in many ways, signs, symbols, videos, books, visions, dreams, speaking in my thoughts, I mean the amount of information I began to learn in the small amount of time was overwhelming. If you know the history of God, although he does answer some prayers immediately, God takes a long time to do things because God's time is perfect timing. Things are seasonal and as you know seasonal changes take a long time. So for God to be feeding me all this information so fast, I was just overwhelmed but at the same time excited he was speaking to me. I even took my followers' suggestion and started a blog but also thanks to my cousin because she inspired me to create one since she had her own to begin with. As I began to send my blogs out, I would get a bigger response and more feedback than I ever have since I started.

One day as I was sitting at the table having a conversation with my Aunt I started to have flashbacks and realized every time I was writing positive messages, I was at the lowest points in my life. My best writings came when I was in my most painful moments and in my darkest hours. I then realized that entire time of going through all those tough times, God was using my pain to serve my purposes and one of my purposes is to share this book with the world. Things began to make perfect sense once I sat down and replayed everything in my head. When you are moving forward in life, you can't connect the dots because the dots aren't there yet but once you replay certain events in your head the dots start to connect. See that time when I had no job, no car, and little money, I call that my "sit down period". Those few months was when God wanted me to himself. Just me and him, no distractions, no connection with the outside world, nothing but me and God spending one on one INTIMATE TIME. God had me practicing my purpose without me realizing it and we were developing our relationship in which I learned so much about him. The closer I got to God the less people I was speaking too. I would literally text 25 plus people a day and that number dropped to maybe 5-6 people and some days I wouldn't speak to anyone. God was not only eliminating people from my life but he told me you can't take everyone on this journey you are about to go on. I was lonely many days and it was very difficult because I was so use to speaking to so many people daily, that being lonely became very uncomfortable. I had to learn patience, consistency, commitment, I could go on but the learning process of this journey is endless. I am still currently on my journey as I write this book but the most important advice I would give is understanding the pain you are going through or went through, God will use it to serve your purpose. God communicates in so many ways but if you are so focused on the pain you will miss not only your purpose but a major blessing. Seek an intimate relationship so you can understand how God works. Once you begin your journey he will speak to you in many different ways, so keep your eyes open and be very focused. This journey gets lonely by the day, so if you are someone who doesn't like to be lonely, you have to get used to it and accept it. Don't fight it and force conversations because God needs you alone so he can work on you. You will lose people you love very dearly, he will show you why certain people don't belong in your life and some people will take it to heart but you have to understand God is more important than a friend. He will also put you through many tests to get you ready so be prepared to pass the test. If God wants that friend in your life at that moment then God will make sure that friend will be there but you can't take everyone on your journey. Temptation will come your way to stop your progress but God will protect you as long as you do your part and fight it. If you slip up and make a mistake do not drown yourself in self-pity, just pick yourself up and start where you fell at. This journey will be very long, hard and uncomfortable but I promise it's a beautiful journey once God gives you understanding and begins to speak to you. If you noticed through my story I only wrote positive messages when I was in pain or going through a rough time. When I was happy with life, I never wrote but I feel like that was God's way of telling me that I need to write when life is good as well because God doesn't always want to bring you to rock bottom to help others. Sometimes we get distracted when life is good and we are happy again but now that I am aware of that, I will write at all times and with all my emotions. Make sure when God gives you your purpose and begin to bless you, do not get distracted or God will pull you down to rock bottom to remind you what you need to be doing. I call this life long journey "The Valley" because in the valley you will experience test, trials and tribulations, battles, distractions, darkness, light, and many other things. The start to the valley is the first step because you made the choice to take the journey to seek God. The journey through the valley is the most important step because that's where you learn everything you need to prepare for what God is trying to teach you. Reaching the mountain is the reward for making it through the valley and at the top of that mountain, God is waiting for you. I wish you the best in your Valley and trust me it is not easy at all but it's worth it in the end, just focus on the finish line.

VIII

Sacrifice a Little for a Lot

The definition of sacrifice is "something you give up, usually for the sake of a better cause." When I hear the word sacrifice, the first thing that comes to mind is my mother. That is one word that I can confidently say that is a trait built in my mom's character. For as long as I could remember, my mother exemplified sacrifice every single day for her kids. Even if that meant sacrificing her happiness to make sure we were happy. Now although I understand that isn't the ideal thing to do, it taught me a powerful lesson about life in general. If you want certain things in life you are going to have to sacrifice something for a bigger and better purpose. There were times where my mother would sacrifice her food just so my sister and I could eat a good meal. There were times where I'm sure my mother wanted to buy some clothes just to treat herself for working so hard, but I've never seen my mother go shopping for clothes just because she wanted to. She sacrificed her desires to make sure my sister and I had clean clothes on our backs at all times. The problem with many of us is we are not willing to sacrifice for our future. We are not willing to sacrifice partying, we aren't willing to sacrifice time with our friends, we aren't willing to sacrifice our pleasure of the present just so we can have a better future. We all want to live these lifestyles or want nice things in life but aren't willing to sacrifice our time and aren't willing to go through the pain to get it. In order to reach any goal that you truly want, you have to be willing to sacrifice. I was watching the story of Paul and during the movie there were two men getting whipped for preaching the gospel. As they were getting whipped they were thanking God because for them it was an honor that they were chosen to be taking the whips for God because they understood God chose them for a greater purpose. They sacrificed their body and pain because they knew the reward at the end would be worth it. No matter what you want to do in life, if you want to be great at something, you have to be willing to sacrifice something for the greater good. I'll never forget my mother bought me an Xbox for my birthday but there was an important bill that needed to be paid. I already unwrapped the Xbox and was excited but my mom asked for it back because she needed the money to pay for a bill. I could tell she was hurt because she didn't want to take that gift away on my birthday because she wanted to see me happy more than anything. As she explained why she needed to take the Xbox back, she promised she would get me another one as soon as she got the money. I gave the Xbox back and I felt no negative emotions towards her or the fact I didn't get an Xbox for my birthday. My mom sacrificed her entire life to make sure I had what I needed, so how dare I get upset I didn't get an Xbox for my birthday. I smiled and looked at my mom and told her "it's fine, you don't have to get me another Xbox, and I'll be OK". Whatever she had to do with the money was a lot more important than a materialistic game that will only last a couple of years. The lesson behind her sacrifice would stick with me for a lifetime and I am a lot more grateful for that than a video game. For those of you who are students and you want to graduate you will have to sacrifice some party time for a diploma. For those of you who want a nice house for your family, you are going to have to sacrifice some free time to put in extra work to get it. For those of you who want to have a better relationship with God, you are going to have to sacrifice your bad habits to obtain good habits.

As a college athlete I had to sacrifice a lot for the things that I wanted to achieve. Many students attend college but never been student athletes. They feel as though college athletes have a great lifestyle and get things easy. Well although that is true in some cases, a lot of people don't understand what college athletes have to sacrifice in order to reach their goals. A normal schedule for me when I was in college was wake up early for class, go to about 2 morning classes, go back home for a small break, long enough to eat a quick meal then head back to an afternoon class. Once the afternoon class was over, go to study hall for an hour and a half, go to the locker room and get ready for practice for two hours. Once we are finished with practice we have to go lift weights or attend yoga for at least an hour. After that we head home and finish whatever homework we didn't complete in study hall or we study things we went over in class while doing our errands we couldn't do during the day; such as wash clothes, or straighten out our living space. We wake up and do it all over again. We would have to sacrifice a lot of our free time to school, sports, and regular responsibilities but we were fine with that because we did it for a greater purpose. We even sacrificed holidays with our families as well.

While many students lived 2-3 hours away at max, a lot of athletes came from other another state and because some of us were in season, we were only able to go home for Christmas break and spring break which was only a few days. So although we did sign up for that type of sacrifice, understand it wasn't easy being a college.

If you want to reach your purpose on earth and you want to become closer to God you have to be willing to sacrifice many things in your life. You have to be willing to sacrifice worldly things, world desires, bad habits, time, money, sleep, food, relationships, even family and you must be willing to sacrifice for the greater good of your own life. You will have to sacrifice your time to pray, you will have to sacrifice food to fast, you will you will have you sacrifice everything negative to turn into a positive for a much greater reward than instant gratification.

IX
Cup of Focus & Pinch of Faith

Focus Focus Focus!!! How many times have we heard this word? Focusing is one of those things that takes hours of practice and sounds simple but it is easier said than done. Life is such a distraction that we fail to realize that it becomes a part of our daily routine. Have you ever sat back and payed attention to how many times you been completing a task and you get so side tracked you forgot what you were doing? The most common example I've seen growing up is being a college student trying to graduate and allowing distractions to either prolong their graduation date or not making it at all. We all have been guilty of it from sacrificing study time to party, hanging out with friends, and allowing personal problems to keep us off course from graduating. We all have been guilty of being unfocused but the problem is being disciplined enough to get back on track and picked up where we left off because once we realize how far off track we are, we begin to become discouraged, which causes many people to give up. Another major distraction going on today is social media and electronics. If you ask me I believe that is the number one distraction today because if you stop to look around, everyone is on their phones. People cannot even focus on simple task such as driving due to the fact that they are distracted by what's going on in their phone or what's going on in the social media world. How many times have you been doing a task and you just so happened to pick your phone up to get on social media or surf around on the internet? As you are entertained on your phone, you look up at the clock and realize how much time went by. We waste hours at a time then, we go into a panic because we were supposed to complete a task but got side tracked by our electronic device. This is such a huge problem that we don't realize how bad this is affecting our lives. What that does is slowly cause us to have a short attention span on things we need to complete which then turns into a bad habit. Many of us don't even have the attention span to fold clothes without stopping to watch TV or get on Facebook or Instagram. Now what if God gave you an assignment to complete? As you know when God ask you to do something it isn't on your time, meaning you cannot take your sweet time to get his purpose done. It must be done at his deadline and he needs your undivided attention or else he will assign someone else to do it. Now stop and be honest with yourself for one second. If God ask you to complete a very important task, would you have the focus to complete that task? I'm sure many are saying yes because since it is God, you can drop everything and give him 100% your focus. Well sorry to inform you it isn't that easy to just drop everything and focus because not only do you have your everyday habits of not being focused but you will have the enemy throwing everything at you to make sure you won't complete God's task. The enemy does not throw things at you that he knows you can resist, he throws things such as your biggest weakness you struggle with on a daily basis. That is one of the many reasons why we do not walk into our purpose in life. We are put on earth for a valuable purpose and sometimes cannot complete that task because we do not choose to focus. We get distracted with some of the smallest and meaningless things that not only distract us from our purpose but destroy our life. Really think long and hard about this because this is such a serious issue that we fail to realize how important this is. Is instant gratification of social media, reality television, partying, gossiping, or spending endless time with your friends worth missing your God given purpose? You must ask yourself, is this helping me towards my purpose? Is this worth missing my purpose for? It is a must that God has our undivided attention because God understands the many distractions on the path to your purpose and without that focus, you can't be reliable to serve his purpose. Now the next question is how do we focus?

One of my favorite focus stories was the advice Kobe Bryant gave to Isaiah Thomas when he explained the focus of a lion when it is ready to attack its prey. The lion has bugs and gnats all over his body and eyes but he is so locked in on his prey that he doesn't get distracted by what's around him. If you get distracted by the small things then you aren't as focused as you think you are. If we all were more like lions just imagined the amount of goals and ground we would cover when finishing a task. I'm pretty sure the lion is aware of the flies and gnats but he is so focused on his mission to catch his prey he will not allow himself to fail because failure doesn't process in its brain. It's not that the bugs aren't bothering the lion but he just isn't allowing it to distract him to the point of losing focus. We must have a lion mentality when it comes to focusing on task that God gives us, especially when it comes to our purposes because that is the whole reason you are put on earth. Now as I stated, it is easier said than done to focus but many people just don't know how to focus the right way. Everyone focuses different but the one thing in common is focus starts with the mind. Focus starts with your mentality by deleting anything out your life that is distracting you from your purpose such as friends, material things, partying, social media or whatever it is that you feel pulls you off track from focusing. You must make time in your day to practice on your purpose and practicing how to focus in every facet of your life. You must ask God to order your steps and ask him to give you the necessary tools to become better at focusing. God will help you but you must do your part and make the right decisions. What has helped me focus in the process of writing this book was isolation. God got me to a point where I was stuck and had less access to the world. I was in a city where it wasn't very busy, I didn't have a car at the time, and didn't have access to friends or people that would distract me. I had no choice to focus on God and my purpose but it also taught what was important and how to make focus such a habit that it becomes second nature. I no longer communicated with the same people, I no longer watch too much television, I began to read more, I began to meditate more, I wasn't on social media as much and I was able to control being on electronics as oppose to picking it up by habit. I am not where I want to be because it is a long process training your mind over and over to focus but I have gotten much better. With God's help, I drove myself to such a desire of focus that I won't allow myself to get off track to the point where I cannot complete my task or my mission for the moment. My focus has been tested many times thus far and although I have gotten sidetracked a bit, I snapped out of it and jumped right back on track.

Understand when God gives you a vision for your purpose many people will not see that vision but it is ok because that is only between you and God. That is where you faith steps in and takes over because when the world says no and goes against what you God has told you, you fall back on your faith. People will not understand and even discourage you but take that as a test because many times when we value someone's opinion and they don't agree or see what you see, we don't feel that support and get discouraged but that too is a part of focus. You must not allow anyone or anything to get in your way and that includes people who don't see your vision. It will even be your own family but if it was for them to understand God would have included them to see your vision as well. Keep that focus and take it as God only wants this between you and him. The enemies' job is to convince you in every way that you shouldn't be completing your purpose. He will throw rejection, fear, doubt, pain and everything negative to stop you, but understand that is a good thing because the enemy only attacks when he feels threatened. Think about it, people and many animals only attack you when they feel threatened. Why is the enemy threatened? Because he doesn't want you to fulfill your God given purpose because you will affect a mass amount of people. It is an honor to be a threat and it means you are on the right track but you must stay focused and not allow the enemy to think he has power over your life. The enemy only has as much power as you give it. The about as a kid many of us were scared of the "boogie man" being under our bed. We were so fearful but we failed to realize that he didn't even exist but our mind gave him so much power that it caused us fear. It is the same thing as adults when the enemy attacks we get fearful and not even realize fear only exist because we give it so much power to manifest in our minds. Failing doesn't exist if you don't allow it to manifest in your mind, self-doubt doesn't exist, and all the things the enemy throws in your way doesn't exist unless you give it power to throw you off track. We don't realize how much power we have within ourselves because we see so many people settle that we accept it as normal. Imagine you right now settling for everything in your future. You settled for a house you didn't want, a partner, a job, a life of mediocre. Would you not feel as though you cheated yourself? Are we not worth more than an average and mediocre life? We were made to do amazing things but one of the reasons we settle is because we choose to not have the focus to achieve our goals and purpose. We think things our too far-fetched but I'm sure at a point in time planes flying was far-fetched, electricity was far-fetched, technology and electronics were far-fetched but look where they are today and how it changed the world. What they all had in common was the focus to achieve their purpose. Don't worry about how you will get there, don't worry about the temporary pain, don't worry about worrying, just trust God and do your part and watch how God moves mountains in your life. You are one decision away from greatness if you choose to focus wholeheartedly. Yes it will hurt, yes you will get tired, yes you will cry, yes life will be pulling you down but it will be worth it in the end. Think about it like as a race. For those who have ran track or been to a track meet, the one thing I noticed about the good runners is they run to exhaustion. Although they are well conditioned athletes, it is still painful for them to use so much energy but while they are running, they aren't worrying about the pain, they aren't distracted by the crowd, they aren't worrying about who is next to them because they are racing against themselves. They are so focused on the finish line, they don't let the pain distract them or slow them down. Those who focus on the pain more than the goal will never win. The finish line is right there and the reward is worth more than the hell you went through to get it, so keep stay focus, run your face to the end and don't lose sight of the finish line.

X

Accountability

Although I have learned many great lessons throughout my life, one of the GREATEST lessons my mother taught me was self-accountability. No matter what problem I faced or issue I had with someone, my mom always asked the question "what did you do to contribute to the outcome?" She drilled it in my head so often that it would become part of my daily thinking; I am more than grateful because that one lesson has took me so far in life. Have you ever heard the saying "Take a look in the mirror"? Well having self-accountability is one of the most powerful tools one can possess because it shows that you have the ability to take responsibility for your own actions. Which translates into changed behavior but a lot of people have a very difficult time taking responsibility for their actions because they never take self-accountability into consideration. What most people do is place the blame on everyone else taking the responsibility off of them and never seem to be the problem in any situation. In their mind it was always someone else's fault. Those individuals who think in that manner are very lost and will live a sad life if they do not find it in themselves to change their selfish ways of blaming others. Even when I found myself in situations where the other person was mostly at fault, I still looked at myself and asked "what could I have done to have a better outcome on that situation?" 90% of the time, the end result of a problem is not solely one person's fault because even if the other person contributed 1% to the problem, they still contributed in some form or fashion. One of the reasons people are living mediocre lives is because they blame others for where they are in life. They blame their friends, former teachers, parents, they blame everyone except themselves, which caused them not to change because they never saw themselves as the problem. In their minds they were never the reason for their failures but in actuality, not holding yourself accountable is a failure in itself. I was fortunate enough to have great examples of self-accountability in my life.

I've been playing sports a long time. I grew up playing baseball, football, and basketball became my first love. One of the things all my coaches had in common was holding the players accountable for their actions. From my middle school basketball coach to my college basketball coaches, they all held their players accountable when they made mistakes. Every coach gave us a set of rules to abide by and in order for us to continue playing or not be punished, we had to abide by all the rules. How my coaches held us accountable was they kept their word no matter what even if they didn't want to. If my coach said do not be late for practice or we will run sprints and we actually end up showing up late for practice then we would run sprints as punishment. There were times my coach said he didn't want us to run but he had to hold us accountable and he did that by keeping his word. See by holding us accountable he was teaching us a lesson to take responsibility for our mistakes. If we did not want to be punished, all we had to do was follow the rules by going to class on time, come to practice on time, complete your school work, and if we didn't do those things then we had no one to blame but ourselves. What that forced us to do was be responsible, take a look in the mirror and if we did make a mistake understand that it was our fault for making that mistake. Those mistakes translated over into real life so if we were late for work or didn't study for a test, we took responsibility for such and accepted whatever consequences came with our actions. Another very important lesson one of my coaches taught was holding others accountable too. One day he walked into practice and said "from here on out, If a player is late to practice or a game, all his roommates will run sprints." Now the first thing that popped up in my head was why should I be responsible for another grown man? He is an adult and needs to man up to take care of himself. At first I didn't understand why my coach would want us to do that but as time went on, everything made more sense. My coach didn't want us to play babysitter but what he was doing was teaching us to hold our teammates accountable as well. My coach was holding us accountable but he also wanted us to hold each other accountable because if one person messed up, it affected the entire team. The common goal was so much bigger than us and in order for us to be great, we all had to help each other out for the greater good of the team. That one lesson translated over into making sure we all went to class on time, making sure if someone needed help with their work, we got it done, and even waking everyone up at the same time so we could show up to practice and games together. What that also did was bring us closer together because now we all had a common goal of not only winning but making sure we are on top of our assignments we wanted everyone to do good because we invested so much time and energy into each other. That bond brought us even closer not just as teammates but as brothers and friends.

With that being said a lot of us have many friends throughout our lifetime but the older we get, the more we realize it is extremely rare to have a genuine friendship. If you have two true friends then you are a blessed individual because great friends don't come by every day. One of the greatest qualities a friend can possess is holding you accountable. Just as my teammates did, it taught us to hold our friends accountable as well. A great friend will hold you accountable and tell you what you need to hear instead of what you want to hear. The difference between a friend who picks at everything you do and one who holds you accountable is that they truly care and want the best for you. One of the true test from my teammates that turned into great friends was I told them I was aiming for a 3.5 GPA or higher this semester but during the semester there were times I didn't feel like going to class. They held me to my word and told me to go to class and stressed how I couldn't get that GPA if I missed class. That is what great friends do, they hold you to your word, even when you slack because they care to see you do well. Ladies, when you go out Saturday nights and are too tired to go to church on Sunday but your friends make sure you get up for church and get there on time, those are great friends. Even when you take your walk with God, it is necessary to have accountability partners that will help you to make sure you remain on the straight path to God. Have you ever been on the walk with God and without even realizing, you begin to backslide further away from your path? That is where your accountability partner comes into action because things we do out of old habits and we don't even realize we are slowly backsliding into our old selves. Imagine having three single ropes twisted together to make one giant rope, the more single ropes you have to combine the largest rope, the stronger it will be. It is the same thing with your accountability partners, the more you have, the stronger you all will become but they have to be quality partners. Remember quality over quantity is the most important thing as well. Accountability isn't just a one lane road, it is so broad from holding yourself accountable, holding your friends accountable, and even holding your partner in a relationship accountable.

Holding your partner accountable is something I don't hear often and little to none to be honest. How many people can honestly say they hold their partner accountable? Before we get into a relationship with someone, we have a set of standards and rules of what we will and what we won't accept. The problem is the deeper we get into the relationship, the more we allow the other person to bend the rules for the sake of "love". The love word gets thrown in there so quickly it overpowers what the other person has done. One standard I think we all can agree on is that we will not tolerate disrespect within a relationship. That includes calling each other names, cheating, being dishonest for selfish reasons, belittling your partner, physical abuse and the list continues. 99% of the time your partner will say "I believe in the same thing so you have my word I will not disrespect you." We then tell our partner "if you disrespect me, I will remove and distant myself from you." Now fast forward past the honeymoon phase because everything is butterflies and rainbows during the honeymoon phase. Somewhere down the line one partner disrespects the other by cheating for example. Now what many of us do is forgive the person for cheating which is good because forgiveness is extremely important in order to move on and get passed it. Where many people go wrong is we forgive but forget to hold our partner accountable and what that turns into is a cycle of disrespect because you didn't hold your partner accountable to their word the first time they disrespected you. What we do is forgive and move past it so easily or we don't give our partner enough time to be consistent because we let them back in so soon. They then disrespect you again by name calling or doing something else, in which you become more upset but you still forgive again and the cycle continues until you are fed up with the disrespect in the relationship. Now is the other partner wrong for disrespecting you throughout the relationship? Absolutely, but did you stop to ask yourself how did you contribute to the problem? It is partially your fault because you didn't hold your partner accountable the very first time you were disrespected. Let me put it into a different perspective for you, if a bully came up to you every day and said "Hey I'm going to punch you in the face at 3:00 PM." But the bully doesn't show up at 3:00pm. Every day for the next week he says the same thing but never shows. Are you going to take that bully serious? Probably not because he didn't keep his word and gave empty threats. That is the same exact thing many of us do with our partner by giving them empty threats. We tell them "hey if you cheat I am going to remove myself" but never removed yourself from the situation. If you never remove yourself and hold your partner accountable, do you think your partner will take you serious? When I say remove yourself, that doesn't necessarily mean break up or don't give a second chance but give the relationship space and make them see how life would be without you if they continued to not keep their word. Many of us give so many chances by the time we try to hold our partner accountable it's too late because they don't take us serious. You must hold your partner accountable immediately to show the person you are serious and in fact they will respect your word because they know you would keep it by following through with action. Again words are nothing without action and if you do not hold your partner accountable by action then all you did was waste a word. We worry about so many other things, such as the time and energy invested we put into a relationship, how much you love them, or how fearful you are of being alone. You allow all of those questions to influence your decision that you stay and settle for the disrespect without you even realizing it. We all make mistakes because humans are incapable of being perfect. That doesn't mean you quit the relationship so easily but being respected in a relationship is not up for negotiation. Don't allow your partner to pick and choose when they feel like respecting you. It also doesn't have to be a negative situation but also a positive situation as well. If your partner comes up to you and says they have a goal to lose weight and will be a certain weight by the end of the month then as their partner you must hold them accountable to their own word. If they begin to stop working out and get lazy or lack motivation as their partner you hold them accountable and say "Hey babe, let's go to the gym and hit that goal, I know you are tired but I am holding you accountable on your word so let's go for at least 10 minutes." Yes your partner might be mad at that moment but in the long run they will love and respect you because you did it out of love and wanted the best for them. I cannot stress how important it is to not only keep your word but hold your partner accountable to their word. Accountability is through all facets of life even from a parent's perspective.

As I stated growing up my mom always taught me holding myself accountable. Looking back I have no choice but to thank her but as I got older and started observing things, I realized all parents don't hold their children accountable. I would see my friends placing blame on other people, walking down a dark path, and just making poor decisions because they never saw themselves as the problem. Either their parents didn't teach them self-accountability or their parents blamed others so much that my friends picked the habit up from them. That gave me the thought of teaching my kids being accountable and start at an early age in order for it to be effective. The thing we have to remember is kids are very intelligent and pick up on things fast, so whatever you do to yourself, the child will do to you and themselves. If you don't hold yourself accountable or your kids then they will not hold you accountable or themselves as well. Parents the same rules apply to holding your kids accountable which is keeping your word. The reason I had a respectable fear for my mother is because I knew if I didn't do whatever she said, she was going to keep her word and punish me. There is only one time I can remember my mom not keeping her word when it came to punishing to me. I was in high school and she told me, if you come home with another bad grade on your report card, I am kicking you out the house. Now although my mom always kept her word, I felt as though my mother loved me too much to kick me out so I knew she could do it but I didn't think she would do it. Report card time rolls around and I had a bad grade. I showed my mom the next morning before school, she handed me a trash bag and said "I need you to be out before I get off work." I then said "Where am I going to go?" She said "I don't know, I guess where all the other kids with bad grades go." Then she leaves for work. Now this was on a school day so I went to school thinking the entire day where am I going to go. School ends and I go home to put all my clothes in a trash bag but before I could finish, my mom comes in and has a talk with me. Although she didn't kick me out, I feared the next time would be a lot worse because she always followed her words with actions. Often times I see parents don't like to discipline their kids because they don't want to hurt them or see them cry. I do understand that because it pains me to see my child cry but if you want the best for your child then you have to hold them accountable when you tell them to do something. The same way when God ask us to do something, we need to do it immediately because delayed obedience is actually disobedience. God doesn't order us to do things when we feel like it but God wants it done immediately. It is the same thing with raising our kids when asking or telling them to do something, they must do it immediately or action should be taken the same way God places action on us. If we tell our child to cut the grass by 12 PM and they don't start until 3 PM, as the parent it is your job to hold your child accountable. We as parents have to remember kids only know as much as you teach them so if you don't teach them the right things, you can't be upset at them or expect them to know what exactly to do. Even common sense is taught so understand the role as a parent is to guide them into the real world accountability. The real world will not be as nice as your parents are so if you aren't holding your kids to your word then not only will they not take you serious but they will disrespect you and you are sending them out into the world unprepared. Sending your child into the real world unprepared is a failure as a parent, this is a very important lesson. Again I understand how hard it is to discipline your children because you hate to see them sad, hurt, or angry but it's only an investment for a better future.

XI
The Value of Appreciation

I know you hear this a million times but appreciate the little things in life and don't take anything for granted. As a matter of fact we hear it so much that we take that phrase for granted. There are a lot of things in life that we should step back and fully appreciate from having a job, to being in school, great friends, great family, even smaller things like clean air, water, and food on the daily. Some of us have been having these things for so long that we expect it instead of appreciating it. I'll give you an example, if your partner brings you lunch or flowers every day for a year and the next year they don't do it as much, instead of thanking that person for even taking the time out to bring you something, most people would complain about them not doing it as much because now you're expecting it instead of appreciating it in the first place. If you have someone in your life whether it be a parents or friends that will do things for you, appreciate them because there is someone out there praying for the things that you are receiving now that you don't fully appreciate it. We are all guilty at times and we wait until we lose it for us to remember how much we appreciated it. As you all know the flooding and tragedies in Houston, TX from hurricane Harvey has caused people to lose their cars, homes, clothes, families, and literally everything except the clothes on their back. Now from a far we see this and we feel the compassion to help or feel their pain. The one thing that happens after you help or even feel their pain is you get to sleep in your bed the next day and wake up to live your life. When those people wake up, that is their REALITY now. Not just a bad day for them or bad week but their REALITY for a good amount of time. Some are waking up in shelters, some are waking up on the street, and some aren't even waking up at all. One woman was on the phone calling for help and as she was talking to the person on the other side of the phone, the water began to rise to a point where her kids began to start drowning and she didn't know which child to save because she was in shock. So she cried and screamed and begged for someone to come help but it was too late. The family ended up drowning and lost their lives over the phone as no one could rescue them. Now here we are complaining about not wanting to go to work because it's a Monday and on the other side here is a woman who is watching her kids drown right before her very eyes and knows her last moments of life are slowly ticking away. Can you even fathom watching your kids drown and you can't save them? As the parent your job is to protect your child and you watch them take their last breath as helpless as could be. No one deserves to go through that tragic situation so yes, life sucks sometimes and life isn't fair all the time, but if you have something to be thankful for please focus on that rather than what you don't have because it can all be taken away and that very thing you were complaining about is now gone along with a million more problems.

You would be surprised by how much happier and positive your life would be if you took the time to appreciate the small things in life. Just the basic things that we receive such as air, clean, water, a roof over our head, somewhere to lay our head at night, and food. When you are thankful for the smallest things in life, you appreciate the bigger things even more because you understand they are a privilege to have. I understand we all get caught up into wanting a better life for ourselves but how can we value a better life if we don't appreciate the one we have right now? We have to stop complaining about going to work on Monday's and be thankful for having a job, we must stop complaining about our poor situations and find the light in a bad situation. We must stop complaining about not having the car we desire and be thankful that we have a working car that gets us to our destination every day. I can tell you from experience I've taken the city bus to school and work in extremely hot weather, rainy weather and I would have been thankful to been in any type of car at that time. Even if you look at many people serving time in prison, when they get out of prison one of the first things they do is look around the world and appreciate everything they hear, see, smell and can touch. They have a whole new appreciation for the world because their freedom was taken from them. When was the last time you just went outside and appreciated the basic foundations of this world? Even appreciating people as well such as your parents, siblings, co-workers, or anyone close to you. Sometimes we have been treated well by our friends and family for so long, we expect them to be that way and forget to appreciate them because everyone isn't as loving as they are. When I was a child, my mom would always say "Aren't you glad you have me as a mom?" I would say "of course" but I said that because it was my mom and I didn't understand what she fully meant when she asked me that question. Growing up, I thought all mothers were the same as far as loving their children and doing everything they needed to make sure their children had the best chance at succeeding in life. As I got older, I begin to see other kids with their parents and started to realize how all kids and mothers didn't have a great relationship. In fact, some kids even hated their mother or their mother hated their own children. I couldn't understand why, especially how I was raised so as I got older I started to appreciate my mother a lot more. Even though parents are supposed to do everything in their power to make sure their children have the best chance at life, a lot of parents were not doing their job and my mother did everything in her power and more to make sure I had a good life for the future. So when she would ask the question "aren't you glad you have me as your mother" when I got older, I was so appreciative that even my answer had more feelings to it because I understand how much she has affected my life just by simply being my mother. Yes we want to be at the top of the job, yes we want the nicest car and house but if you want to appreciate it you have to go through the process to get it.

Now today let at least 5 people know how much you appreciate them no matter how big or small and let God know what you are grateful for because life itself is a gift. Love & Positivity.

XII

Releasing Your Emotions

Communication is key. How many times have you heard that phrase? How many times have you heard of a relationship or friendship that had serious issues because of communication? I have heard this a million times where communication was the number one reason for breakups, loss of friendships, and confusion in many areas of life. Communication is very underrated. I thought I knew what communication was until I got older and started experiencing life. Growing up as a young male communication has been one of the biggest hurdles in many lives, especially in relationships. As a kid, a lot of males were taught to hold in their feelings or not be so emotional by society. Men are telling their boys to "stop crying and suck it up" or "you are a man, men don't cry, we are tough". Well, those statements are part of the reason why most men do not know how to communicate and why we bottle up so many emotions.

When we try to communicate or express our pain we get labeled as "soft" which deters us from expressing ourselves. This also encourages us to keep our emotions within. Although I am speaking from a male's perspective, some women have issues communicating as well. For right now, I will speak from a male's point of view mainly because I feel this is a serious issue for a lot of men. Not only at home, but influences such as friends, other family members or even coaches discouraged emotions. As a child I played multiple sports and what they all had in common from an emotional standpoint is anytime someone showed vulnerability such as crying or hurt, it was deemed as a sign of weakness. We would hear "suck it up, crying is for girls" or "quit being soft and acting like a female". I do understand the logic behind it, but what happens in the real world when you need to communicate and show vulnerability? We do not know how because we have been conditioned by society for so long to mask our emotions. Unfortunately, when the time comes, we express it in whatever way we know how. Some men explode, some take it out on other people, some cry, and some hurt other people emotionally, mentally, or physically. Please keep in mind that all men do not respond in a negative manner. I do know men who have different outlets to express themselves such as sports, writing, singing, rapping, drawing, etc. which are all positive methods. However, we MUST learn how to communicate verbally and not only through action. This is necessary because everyone may not understand why we express ourselves the way that we do. What makes sense to us may appear to be irrational to others. For example, if a child goes to school picking on only happy kids, most people only see him being a bully. What some people may not realize is that the kid labelled as a bully lost his parents in a car crash and lives with a grandparent he never sees because they are too busy working. The kid is hurting because his parents are gone and he is jealous of other kids being happy. He may not know how to communicate his pain and is too afraid to admit it for fear of people making fun of him. I am in no way saying that the child is right for being a bully, but most people will not understand his point of view.

Most bullies are also hurting inside themselves. How many times have you wanted to communicate how you truly felt but could not find the right words to do it? How often have you been too embarrassed to say how you felt, but would not for fear being judged or made fun of? We, especially as men, need to stop being ashamed of being vulnerable and say what is on our heart. It is important that we take the steps to learn how to communicate the correct way. Growing up, I have witnessed numerous men communicating by either being aggressive, abusive, shut down, fighting and many other ways. Even when we are amongst friends, we may feel strongly about a situation but instead of talking the problem out, we fight because that is the way we were taught to communicate. As a young male it is very difficult to express to your friend that he hurt your feelings. He would likely laugh at you for being soft or make fun of you, so we either fight, pretend that we do not care, or sweep it under the rug. It may seem like you swept it under the rug but what you actually did was add another emotion into the bottle that is already about to explode from past emotions you never released.

I was one of those guys who shut down when it came time to communicate. I was fearful of people laughing about how I felt. Instead of communicating on how I felt I would get an attitude and stop speaking so that I would not have to talk about my feelings. I refused to show my vulnerable side to anyone. I was afraid of someone using my own words against me. I have been in situations where I have communicated deep secrets to someone and they abused my trust. Those situations taught me two things: I should be careful of whom I open up to and to keep my feelings to myself so that it would not happen again. Little did I know I was only making things worse by not communicating, especially when I began to take relationships seriously. One of my go to moves in a relationship would be if I felt a certain way about a situation, I would shut down and not speak to my girlfriend for a few hours or the rest of the day. Instead of just expressing that I was upset about something she did, I would act standoffish with her. I wanted her to guess why I was mad or I would give her the silent treatment. My behavior was very childish and unacceptable. She would then mirror my behavior and become angry. This behavior between the two of us created additional conflict. This type of behavior continued for several years because that was the only way that I knew how to communicate. I am sure you are wondering why did I not just express my feeling. At that time, it was all that I had to offer. You see, if I conveyed how I truly felt, it would have come off as being blunt and rude. I would have been speaking out of anger instead of love. I would have tried to hurt my girlfriend's feelings simply because I felt that she had hurt my feelings. Wanting to do better, I eventually found another way without intentionally hurting her feelings.

    After some time had passed, I finally met someone I genuinely liked. We dated for a while but along the way, there were minor disagreements in which I communicated poorly. I knew my methodology was poor, but I still had not truly put in the required work to get better. I would periodically act out in ways that was within my comfort zone. I tried working on it but continued to struggle with my verbal communication skills. I also tried written communication which was actually better, but my girlfriend was a verbal communicator. Not only did I learn that I had to improve on expressing myself verbally, but when you communicate you have to be mindful of the following:

You have to know who you are communicating with.
That individual's style of communication.
 The best way for them to receive and convey information. A lot of people believe that communicating is yelling at each other, fighting or even sweeping the problem under the rug. As men we have to let go of our fears and vulnerability of communicating. Eventually, we will meet our wives one day. If our communications skills are lacking, the relationship will fail very fast. Trust me, you do not want to be that guy who ended a marriage, lost a girlfriend, or even longtime friend because you did not take the necessary steps to learn how to communicate the right way. This especially applies to marriage. How you communicate with your wife sets the foundation on how your children learn effective communication and coping mechanisms.

XIII

Limitless Boundaries

Have you ever thought to ask, why do we limit ourselves? We live in a society that teaches us to limit ourselves without even realizing it. Even as a kid in first grade, teachers would always ask the question was "what do you want to be when you grow up?" Usually as a child we say a doctor, lawyer, professional athlete, firefighter, I mean the list is endless. Why can't we be more than that? We as people have so much potential within ourselves but we hold ourselves back. Some of our biggest problems is that we limit ourselves and stand in our own way from being great. Let me ask you this, what is stopping one from being an Author, Doctor, Singer, and businessman or businesswoman? Now we don't have to be these things all at once but throughout our lives why not shoot for all those things at some point? Time isn't a problem because you make time for the things you want, so what is the excuse? Think about the Wright Brothers and how many people laughed at them for saying they could build planes. I'm sure they were the only ones that believed they could build a plane but guess what? They did it and proved everyone wrong. God created us so unique and special in which a lot of us don't live into our full potential because we have LITTLE to NO FAITH in ourselves or we have such a deep fear that if we put our all into building our dream and fail that we wouldn't know how to recover from that failure. Most people would rather play it safe by staying complacent because it gives them a level of comfort that won't challenge them to be uncomfortable. Have you reflected and thought how many times you have failed in life thus far? Was failure always bad or resulted in a negative outcome? A lot of the times failure made you better if you learned the mistakes along the way and as a matter of fact, in order for us to grow we must fail and learn from it. Just go back and look at some of the things man has created and tell me we weren't meant to be great. Planes, electricity, internet, cars, and it continues to grow because who on earth would have thought these things were possible? We continue to limit ourselves because we are scared to take chances, we are afraid to fail, we are terrified of people's opinions, and we are petrified of being outside of the norm so we settle for normality. We settle for building others dreams, we settle for spending most of our time working for someone else and have nothing to show for it but a check. We settle for living average lives because it's the "safe" decision to make. God didn't create us to be average or safe. We are made in the image of God so how do we not have greatness inside of us already? Just as God has created everything, we were born to create amazing things in our world but we must do our part and have faith in ourselves. Do you think we have all these far-fetched imaginations for us to keep in our heads and not create them? If you don't think your dreams are far-fetched then you aren't dreaming big enough. Everyone wants that fancy lifestyle but won't settle for greatness. Write down what you are good at, write down your dreams and not just simple ones. Shoot for the sky even if it sounds ridiculous. We are too powerful and have too much potential to let our gifts go to waste. Master your craft, then go change and inspire the world to be better with YOUR gift GOD gave you. Our gifts are so much bigger than ourselves. They were put in us to not only inspire but change the world. So please don't short change and limit yourself in anything because we all have more than one talent but if we limit ourselves we will never tap into our many gifts and use them to their full potential. We just have to be willing to put in the work to do so. Learn as much as possible because knowledge is truly power and if you want this world to be a better place it starts with your gift to the world.

      Limitations and greatness start in your mind. It literally is a mental battle every single day until it becomes a habit and obsession for you to understand what you need to do to believe there are no limitations. One of my favorite people I enjoy watching is Kobe Bryant. Not only because of basketball but his "mamba mentality" on how he approaches everything is incredible. His limitless mentality and expectations for greatness is so powerful that only so many people can fully understand his way of thinking because he approaches things so different. Even at this point I don't fully understand his mentality but what I do understand is in order to be great at many things such as Kobe, some qualities you must possess is being fearless, committed, never provide yourself with excuses, driven, burning desire, obsessed, focused, and many other things. You have to practice these qualities so often and so intensely that it becomes a part of your personality. You have to become obsessed with this mentality to be great. What intrigues me about Kobe is he won't allow his mind to process failure. Often times when many of us are in pursuit of something, we manifest failure in our minds and begin to ask ourselves well what if I don't pass this test? What if I lose the race? What if I don't do well or what if I don't get the job? That is a loser's mentality because you are already preparing your mind for failure instead of success. If you focus on the reward instead of failing then more times than not, you will reach your goal. It starts within your mind first and failure isn't failure if you learn from it. Our greatest lessons come from "failing" so is that really considered failure if that helped you reach your ultimate goal? Quitting is failure, giving up is failure, mediocre is failure, average is failure and anything outside of being your best is failure. Every day is a consistent grind. You don't have time to not feel like doing it, you don't have time to be tired, and you don't have time to do it later, make the choice right now.

  Greatness is a lifestyle at which should start at an early age. It isn't something you do for a day, a week, a month or a year but you do it forever. Greatness becomes a habit and a lifestyle that you live in every aspect of your life forever. For those who have kids, plant that seed of greatness early but in order for you to teach them greatness you must speak its language. You must go through your process to become great and if you are reading this book then it is not too late no matter what age you are. Start now so you can become better for your kids, so you can teach them to be great early and they won't make some of the same mistakes you made. I have a son who is currently four years old and the things he has taught me at his age are things I will use forever as an adult. At the age of two my son was able to learn the entire alphabet, learn his colors, count to 50, learn his planets, and learn numerous amounts of shapes from the basic ones such as circle all the way to rhombus to parallelogram. He learned facial features and even a few nursery rhymes. At the age of three he learned how to say his alphabet backwards, he has learned how to spell some words, he has learned how to write down the words, and even gets upset if he messes up on a letter. At the age of three he learned his planets and began to find interest in the solar system. Now for those who don't have kids that is not common for a child at that age to learn all of those things in that amount of time or to learn those things at that age period. Credit goes to his grandmother and mother for teaching him all of those things but what that taught me is never limit your child or yourself because you don't know what you are capable of learning or what your child can learn. Most people wouldn't even think to teach a child that but because she did, his ability to learn and retain information is amazing. Planting that seed of greatness in him early will allow him to not limit his potential for learning. Who are we to say what a person should or shouldn't know at a certain age? That is because we limit ourselves from greatness because we hold ourselves to the world's standards instead of ourselves. If we teach our kids, or grand-kids at an early age then it will turn into a lifestyle for them to the point where they will be great at many things. It will be contagious to other family members, friends, and anyone who is in our path. It starts with you because you have to get procrastination out of your life, you have to kill laziness, you have to kill excuses out of your life, you have to kill cheating, you have to kill quitting, you have to kill your old mentality and create a new one. The only difference between you and other people that are great is the mentality, focus and execution. The greatness is already in you, but if you change your mentality the focus and execution will follow right behind it. You have one life to be great to change your life and your families' lives. You are waiting for greatness to fall in your lap but you have to go get it.

Note From The Author

First and foremost I want to give all honor & glory to the highest GOD. I want to thank my entire family and friends for supporting me throughout this journey. I want to thank anyone who has impacted me in a positive way, anyone who has ever given me advice, and anyone who has never given up on me. I want to thank everyone who pushed me or gave me the idea to even write a book. I want to thank everyone who has helped me edit and gave me constructive criticism for this book. My reason for writing this book was too solely to help the world. Any inspiration, motivation or self-help that you gained from this reading was the purpose for writing this book. The younger people who have yet to experience life, take these words with you and get a head start on life. You are the future and we need every single one of you. Those who are in their 20's such as myself, take these words and apply it to your life or to help a friend. Our 20's could be our hardest years but if we all work together for a common goal to make the world better I believe we can do it. The fact of you reading this book says you believe it as well. For the adults 30 and above it is never too late to change and improve. Yes a lot of you all have made mistakes you are paying for now but the fact of you reading this book says you want to be better. That desire to be better is all the fuel you need to change no matter what age you are. I chose not to complicate the reading by expanding my vocabulary or have hidden messages because I want everyone who reads this to have clarity on all the messages and advice I am trying to convey. We all were born with greatness inside of us but only you can allow that greatness to flourish. Keep supporting and Thank you for taking this journey with me.

      Sincerely yours,

         Ryan Weems

Email: Rweems1109@gmail.com

Facebook: Ryan King Weems

Rest In Peace

Tera Weems

Brian Brown

Made in the USA
Middletown, DE
23 October 2018